# SONGS OF AN UNCAGED PARROT

# SONGS OF AN UNCAGED PARROT

## Some Curious Cases of an Upright Police Officer

Rajendra Shekhar
IPS (Retd.)

Former CBI Director and Former DGP, Rajasthan

Konark Publishers Pvt Ltd
New Delhi

**Konark Publishers Pvt. Ltd**
206, First Floor,
Peacock Lane, Shahpur Jat,
New Delhi 110 049
Phone: +91-11-41055065
e-mail: india@konarkpublishers.com, us@konarkpublishers.com
website: www.konarkpublishers.com



ISBN: 978-81-949286-8-3

Edited by Dipali Singh
Cover Design by Sanjeev Mathpal
Cover image ©Shutterstock
Typeset by Saanvi Graphics, Noida
Printed and bound at Thomson Press (India) Ltd

*To my Father*

# Contents

# Introduction

## *Walking the Thin Line*

When working in positions, like I did, as Director, Intelligence Bureau (IB) and Director, Central Bureau of Investigation (CBI), the winding up process routinely goes beyond working hours. This created an eternal conflict with my fiendish need for a daily physical workout. To ensure that I fitted this in my schedule, I would walk from office to my allotted residence in New Delhi, letting my driver take the car home.

One evening in the twilight of a wintry day in 1990, on my vigorous walk back home, I sensed, rather than saw, a car slowing down beside me. Immediately, my sleuth instinct kicked in, making me wary. The car kept cruising along for a while and then overtook me as I walked on the pavement. Without breaking my stride, I gave a cautiously curious glance at the intruder and to my relief, recognized M.K. Narayanan. I smiled and he beamed back, then opened his window and politely but firmly asked me to climb into his car. Partly for the sake of his seniority but mainly because of the bonhomie we enjoyed, I did.

M.K. Narayanan, Director, IB, was my neighbour in the North Block offices in New Delhi's Central Secretariat. We had a very congenial relationship and would informally walk into each other's office for a friendly chat or for official consultations several times a day, if required. Even our official residences were on the same road, on lanes almost opposite each other. So, it was only inevitable that our paths would at times cross on the way home, too.

He was in a sombre mood that evening. He said, 'Shekhar, do you realize that you are taking a big risk by walking alone? The IB has received reliable information that a group of terrorists has entered Delhi with the intention of causing harm to VIPs, and you may be one of the targets.'

Now, I was fully aware of the resolve of a person called Jinda to complete his unfinished agenda—of causing fatal bodily harm to some of the senior officers entrusted with the investigation and supervision of the Ludhiana dacoity case. The incident had taken place in 1987. Jinda was the confidant of Sukhdev Singh, head of the Khalistan Commando Force (KCF), the militant organization based in Punjab. The KCF had looted cash worth more than Rs 5 crore from the vaults of the Punjab National Bank in 1987 and I, as the Joint Director, CBI (Special Investigations), had spearheaded the probe. This case is the basis of a later story in this book.

I began to reply to Narayanan, saying 'If you are talking of...'

He interrupted me, 'Not Jinda. My memory is still pretty good though I may be older than you...he got caught for the Vaidya murder case and is in the Pune jail on death row. All the same, a terrorist's unfinished agenda doesn't die with him—the fact remains that it's too risky for you to walk like this in the open without a guard...'

I deferred to a senior officer's sane advice and began to go home in my car, replete with my security detail, and confined my evening constitutional to the compound of my spacious residence. The pleasing side effect was the grateful reaction of Mrs Shekhar as she was now spared the scary vision of a husbandless car entering the premises of 22, Tughlaq Crescent.

Why I bring up this episode to start my narrations here is because it defines the DNA of my existence, my triple helix, so to say: my solid work ethic, the balance between thinking with the head and listening to my heart, and my ever vigilant wife. I've walked the thin line between them all my life. It's been quite a tightrope, but I'm still walking at 87 albeit with a walking stick, as upright as can be.

As I play possibly my last innings in book writing, it would be appropriate to refer to my icon, Don Bradman, the greatest batsman the world has witnessed. In a way, I'm taking a leaf out of his book. When he was on the verge of reaching an astonishing career average of 100 in Test cricket, he announced that he was retiring from the longest format of the game. He required just four runs to reach the milestone. His farewell game (against England at The Oval on 14 August 1948) was hugely anticipated by the entire crowd. But destiny had planned something else for him—he was bowled for a second-ball duck in that innings! Though he missed this mark by a whisker, he was not tempted to postpone his retirement and stuck to his resolve despite several people, including powerful ones, asking him to play one more Test. As a result, his batting average stands at a tantalizing 99.94, still by far the highest ever average in Tests, a record that many say will never be surpassed.

While I am nowhere near as accomplished as The Don, this book is cast in the same mould in that this may well be my last song. And like The Don, I don't know how many runs I will score but I'm determined to do my best without bothering to keep score. Like him too, I hope people remember me as the officer who refused to be caged by records and the powers that be.

# I

# Role Model

## Prologue

As a schoolboy at Mayo College, the prestigious boarding school in Ajmer, Rajasthan, I had sat for the Joint Services Test, my aim being to join the Indian Air Force. I got through with flying colours in the written examination but failed on medical grounds. However, since I had done well in the written and physical tests, I was given a grace period of six months and was asked to 'beef up' a bit and come back if I wanted to join the defence services. Meanwhile, I also applied to St Stephen's College in New Delhi for graduation studies but that, too, would take seven months before I could join. I had ample time on my hands to make my choice in the small town of Tonk in Rajasthan where my father was posted as a civil servant at that time. There was not much to do and I had no friends in Tonk because most of my life had been spent in the hostel at Mayo.

I was at a loose end and would have spent my vacation mulling over my choices again and again, but for the Tonk Club, with its tennis court and well-stocked library. And it had the most interesting members, one of whom, in fact, inspired me to tie up a loose end in my life—my choice of career. I would get to know this gentleman several months later, though I saw him often enough in the library.

Most of the club members were unenthusiastic about the library but none more than Masoom, the Nawab of Tonk designate, my senior at Mayo, who took me under his wing and introduced me to club life in Tonk. He was an exceedingly friendly soul, an active member of the club, and he welcomed me with open arms—but he was a hard core 'outdoor' type.

It took me a month or so to escape Masoom's sphere of influence to fulfil my love for reading. On the very first day, I ran into a gentleman (or rather, saw him in the distance because we were the only two in the cavernous hall of the library) who seemed to be as avid a reader as I was. He sat at a desk pouring over some manuscripts and looked as if he'd been sitting there for days. He looked up at me, seeming slightly surprised to see someone else in the library, and then went back to his books. Subsequently, I frequently saw him in the library when I was selecting my reading material. We began to nod at each other and once or twice exchanged a few words about our reading preferences. That was all. I never even tried to get to know his name but I was instantly drawn to him and the feeling was mutual I think, or it might have been my teenage imagination running wild.

Still, there was no denying the fact that even in other spaces of the club, like the tennis court, we would gravitate towards each other. Presumably, our minority status in the multitude of 'outdoor types' had sparked this camaraderie. Or that's how I explained it to myself at least. That there was much more to it would be revealed to me in the coming month.

It just so happened under less than pleasant circumstances. One day, while fooling around with Masoom on the roof of his *haveli* (family manor), I jumped over the parapet on to what I thought was a terrace but miscalculated the distance and fell all the way to the ground. Luckily, my fall was broken by a mound of soft mud lying there for some ongoing construction. But the accident, nevertheless, resulted in an excruciating back pain for several days that confined me to my bed. That's when I actually met him, my library acquaintance. Out of the blue, this gentleman landed up at our house to commiserate about the accident and to offer to pick up some books for me. My father wasn't at home at the time. Feroze, my father's assistant, was sitting next to me in a chair and I was surprised by his reaction when he saw my visitor. He stood up immediately, a frozen, awestruck expression writ large on his face. The gentleman smiled at Feroze and politely asked him to sit down; then he pulled up another chair and sat near my bed.

He cheered me up for a while, telling me how at my age the injuries I had suffered would heal very quickly and I would be up and about, playing tennis in no time. In fact, he was missing me at the club, he said. I don't think I was very coherent in my replies, since I was so surprised to see him and also confused by Feroze's attitude towards him. After a while, he stood up, shook my hands firmly and warmly and giving me a mock salute, said, 'Young man, you better hurry up and get on your feet. I am longing to beat you in a tennis game.'

Of course, it was just a motivating gimmick. Not that he was too old or anything; he must have been in his late fifties and could very well have been an accomplished tennis player, but I'd only seen him grace the tennis court as a spectator, often in the gallery clapping for the underdog in a match. I recall that when I was playing Masoom, the runaway favourite as the winner of the Tonk Club Tennis Cup, in the finals, my library friend had clapped and cheered from the gallery as I gave a good fight to Masoom who was quite shocked at my unexpected and doughty challenge. So much so that in the last set, his game came apart and I actually won the match!

When my visitor left after gently smiling at my father's assistant, Feroze sat down heavily on the chair vacated by him and said, 'Wah, you have some fancy friends!'

I replied, 'He's not really a friend; actually I don't even know his name. Why do you call him fancy? Who is he?'

'What a man he is, *Bhaisahib, kyaa admi hain*! Don't you know who he is?' He stood up again as if in reverence to my visitor. Seeing his approximation of a standing ovation, which was incomprehensible to me, I asked him to expand on the reasons for his effusive praise of the man. He mumbled something laudatory again and I could only wait for him to recover from his daze.

Finally, he became more lucid and explained, 'There are many instances of his bravery but let me tell you about the incident that made Sunder Lalji a household name in all of Tonk. You won't believe what he did to save the day.' Though his was an emotional rendering of the story sans some details, which I had to later glean from other sources, Feroze's tale matched his build-up.

The story that I narrate here has been added to by the then Station House Officer (SHO) who was involved in the incident and Masoom Ali, my friend from Mayo.

For many centuries, Tonk was ruled by Nawabs and it still continues to have a sizeable Muslim population. After India's independence, it was merged into Rajasthan as a district. Its Muslim rulers had taken pains to maintain communal accord by wholeheartedly participating in Hindu cultural, religious and social functions, as a result of which Tonk was traditionally a haven of communal harmony.

Notwithstanding this, in view of the general climate of distrust and vengeance engendered by the Partition of India, the government authorities had alerted all the sensitive districts, including Tonk. To forestall trouble, they also augmented the district police force with an additional deployment of personnel.

Tension started heating up after Malpura, a subdivision of Tonk, was gripped by communal discord after the Partition. It precipitated so rapidly that the administration had to face a full-scale riot that raged in many areas of the district headquarters. The administration took immediate steps to control the situation. It clamped Section 144 of the Code of Criminal Procedure (CrPC), posted pickets in the more vulnerable mohallas (neighbourhoods), requisitioned more troops and closely monitored developments through the city Circle Officer (CO) and Sunder Lal, the then Deputy Superintendent of Police (DSP), who decided to camp at the city *kotwali* (police station).

The undercurrent of tension, however, did not abate and following sporadic incidents of unrest, it erupted into a ferocious flare-up. The brunt of the violence was faced by a particular section of the town, where the Muslim population was high. DSP Sunder Lal along with the SHO rushed to the spot.

On seeing the approaching police contingent, the warring factions ran back to their own mohallas. Lal cordoned off the area and lined up his men in the street separating the two ghettos. The opposing mobs, deprived of the opportunity to get at each other's throats, congregated in clusters in their own locality and began hurling projectiles—stored for precisely such an eventuality—at each other. And the police force was haplessly caught in the crossfire of the warring groups.

Lal, who was leading his men from the front, moved courageously forward in the face of bricks and stones hurled by the mob. These missiles directly hit him on his chest and face and he was struck by one large brick that caused a deep gash on his cheek. He almost fell down with the blow but despite the pain, he immediately straightened up and resolutely braved the fusillade from both sides, not stopping for a moment to tend to his own multiple injuries. He had a blood-stained uniform, a gashed cheekbone and a bleeding nose very soon but undeterred, he didn't falter from his line of duty. He resolutely continued leading his force, trying to get the two warring factions to calm down and stop the barrage of stones and bricks but there was no letup—even the use of tear gas proved futile. He was now faced with two options—to disperse the mob by firing into the crowd and risking the lives of several 'innocent' civilians or to attack them aggressively with a large contingent of his men wielding lathis (wooden sticks). He knew the second course of action would result in injuries to his men and himself, but being the brave and compassionate officer that he was, DSP Lal decided on a lathi-charge. It had to be a coordinated two-pronged charge, simultaneously conducted in both the mohallas and this action would require more men than he had, which meant that he had to call a back-up force.

DSP Lal asked the SHO to repeatedly warn the crowds on his portable mike to disperse, as he waited for the requisitioned force to arrive. When the reinforcements finally arrived, he split up the striking force into two segments for a simultaneous thrust in both directions. The policemen were instructed to force the rowdies into their mohalla precincts, back into their houses, and to confiscate the projectiles.

Opting for the lathi-charge rather than firing at the mobs showed Lal's courage and forbearance in the line of duty and could already be deemed heroic—yet his real heroism was yet to emerge.

As he was about to give the go-ahead signal for the lathi-charge, an unforeseen incident put a spanner in his plans. At that precise moment, an old woman who found herself in the wrong side of the war, decided to dash across, back to her side of the divide. For her age it was rather a rash decision and even before she could reach the police cordon in the middle, someone in the opposing camp threw a solid brick right at her head, a hard blow near her left ear. She stumbled and fell as her vegetable basket flew out of her grip and its contents sprayed all over the street.

DSP Lal did not hesitate even for a moment, his compulsive compassion impelling his next few actions. Rushing to her, he bent over her writhing frame to form a human shield over her body. Even as other missiles flew all around and hit Sunder Lal again and again, he didn't flinch. He ordered his team to pick her up from under his protective body and put her in the police jeep, then asked the SHO to take her at once to the hospital for treatment.

The SHO hesitated because the jeep was the only available vehicle capable of negotiating the narrow entry points of the two warring ghettos. And it was the only way out for Lal to exit if things got out of control. But Lal was not thinking of anything except the old lady's safety—he noticed that the woman had lost consciousness, so he firmly pushed the SHO towards his jeep and told him to stop dithering and go. He was to return only after he had ensured that she was under proper care at the hospital.

It was only then that the battered Lal ordered the two-pronged lathi-charge. Thankfully, his strategy worked. It resulted in not much injury to his men, as the crowd had seen the officer take prompt action to save the old lady, and this probably evoked some remorse about what had happened. One can only guess how Lal's courageous compassion might have tamed the wild beast inside some of the people in the mob but, eventually, they gave up and went back to their houses without too much of force having to be used. Calm was then restored to the mohallas. When news spread of the situation settling down in this sensitive area of the town, peace spread like a fire from this spark lit by Lal to all of the city of Tonk. At least for that night, a heroic act had prevailed over the surging communal hatred.

Meanwhile, DSP Lal arranged for the injured to be treated, before he got his own wounds looked at. In the morning, after life in Tonk got back to normalcy and calm, thanks to the unrelenting efforts of the administration and the 'peace committee', he went to the hospital to see the old lady. His cheekbone had been bandaged, his face was swollen and his strapped chest ached as he breathed cautiously. Some media men were waiting for him there but he refused to talk to them because he didn't hanker for publicity or sympathy—what had driven his actions was his innately compassionate nature. His personal pain and discomfort remained subordinate to his compelling urge to help another human being in distress.

Beaming relatives of the old lady welcomed him and one of them identified Lal to her, '*Ye Diptee Sahib hain* (This is the Deputy Sahib). *Inhone aapki jaan bachai* (He saved your life).' She looked at Lal and smiled gratefully. Then in a choked voice, she said, '*Beta, Allah tujhe barkat de aur ooncha audha de* (May Allah give you prosperity and you reach a higher post). *Meri dua se tu jaldi hee shahr kotwal bane.* (With my blessing you should soon become the SHO).'

Her blessing was followed by a stunned silence and the incumbent SHO looked apologetically at his boss, in genuine embarrassment because it was a demotion that the old lady was unwittingly wishing on Lal. And yet the old lady was only echoing the public perception. In the public eye, the SHO is the most visible and powerful police functionary because he heads the police station.

DSP Lal broke the awkward silence with a hearty laugh and the others, taking his cue, joined in. Lal said, '*Shukriya ammijaan. Khuda aapko sahi salaamat rakhe.* (Thank you, mother. May God keep you healthy and safe).'

How did Feroze know about this story? This question was uppermost in my mind. And then he told me what the reason was. It was because he was also present in the hospital at that moment and had stood quietly on the edge of the old lady's bed, overcome by emotion. She was his grandmother.

Her blessings struck their intended mark as Sunder Lal was among the first few state officers to be inducted into the Indian Police Service (IPS), thus facilitating his early promotion as a Superintendent of Police (SP).

In those growing impressionable years, this story had a deep impact on my psyche, so much so that Sunder Lal became my role model and I can attribute my joining the police force directly to him. Throughout my IPS career, I have tried to live up to his principle of according priority to human life over the hidebound adherence to rules.

# 2

# The Buck Has to Stop Somewhere

*'If you can't stand the heat, get out of the kitchen. The buck stops here...'*

— *Harry Truman*

**Prologue**

When I was transferred to the high-profile district of Udaipur while still in the early years of service, I took it as an endorsement of my 'good work' in Barmer, where I'd been posted during the Indo-Pakistan war of 1965.

And yet, my elation was tempered by the element of immense responsibility the posting entailed. Udaipur also happened to be the district to which Mohan Lal Sukhadia, the then Chief Minister (CM) of the state, belonged. It wasn't as communally charged a place as Tonk, and CM Sukhadia had a 'secular' image, but opposing him was a faction with strong 'rightist' leanings, who were hellbent on embarrassing him.

They had been polarizing the city on some pretext or the other ever since the CM's victory in the elections and when I took charge as SP, the city was charged with these political undercurrents that threatened to explode at the slightest provocation.

When it did, the reason for the sudden eruption was, of all things, a wrestling tournament. While the police had been very watchful during functions of religious significance, this sporting event had not been on their radar as a potential cause of a communal riot. They were caught on the back foot and thus by the time they acted decisively, the violence had taken its toll.

How had a wrestling tournament spiralled out of control? It was the heavyweight category bout between a newcomer and the three-year running champion that sparked off the riot. It was also the chief attraction of the tournament and had drawn a large crowd. The rookie youngster was talented and eventually expected to wear the crown, but that year the stakes heavily favoured the reigning champion.

Even so, a devoted camp gave vociferous support to the youngster, at times drowning out the reigning champion's retinue of followers. As it happened, it had been billed as a communal fight and this fact hadn't been picked up by police intelligence. Vijay Singh, the Hindu challenger, was being pitted against Hanif Mohammad, the Muslim champion.

So when, against all expectations, Singh won the bout, the loser's camp lost no time in rejecting the verdict on the premise that the contest was rigged. The small police contingent present at the spot was able to control the situation, but the animosity was carried by the champion's fans into the city.

About a week later, there was an altercation between two pushcart vegetable vendors, each belonging to one of the two communities that escalated into a knife fight. Hafiz, one of the vendors, slipped and fell down during the scuffle, which saved him from a vicious thrust and there was no serious harm done. However, seeing a chance to cause trouble for the Hindus, Feroze, his assistant, whispered to Hafiz to feign unconsciousness, then put him on the cart and raced away, claiming he was taking Hafiz to the hospital. Instead, he went to the Muslim mohalla, where he stirred up an already angry hornet's nest by claiming that Hafiz had been attacked by a group of Hindus and would have been killed but for his timely intervention in spiriting him away.

Feroze had a reason for grossly exaggerating the incident. He was a cousin of Hanif Mohammad, the wrestler, and had been seething with discontent at Vijay Singh's victory. His community's reaction to the exaggerated claims was immediate. They came out of their houses armed with missiles and hostility. Feroze was a notorious mischief-maker and word spread around that he was up to something, which alerted the Hindus who prepared for retaliation. Before the police got wind of the brewing trouble, it had erupted onto the streets. There were widespread clashes, leaving two dead and many injured in no time at all. The police got the situation under control finally by sunset, but the city was still simmering.

In a district police set-up, the SP is the ultimate arbiter of law and order matters and his competence is largely assessed by 'on the spot' decisions he takes. The buck stops at his desk—as it should. Whereas he can take time to deliberate in other matters, in a law and order situation, his decisions have to be instant, unambiguous and effective.

In this case, the police, caught on the wrong foot as the vegetable vendors' quarrel twisted unexpectedly into a communal conflict, had to take firm charge of the situation. Being a sensitive district, from where the CM hailed, made things worse and our every move was under watch. We decided to clamp a curfew and give 'shoot at sight' orders. We utilized the lull after sunset to douse fires, tend to the injured, strengthen pickets, collect intelligence and to round up suspects.

We had our fingers crossed as we waited in nervous apprehension for the next day, fully aware that once the demon of communal discord is let loose to dance its dance of death and destruction, then even our fire-fighting measures could prove woefully inadequate. It has happened again and again in so many parts of our country, as if the communal fires of the Partition have never really been doused.

I shifted my control room to the city kotwali (police station) during this incident. The first thing I did was to ask for more men on the street. The tension was palpable as I waited for the requisitioned reinforcements to arrive. Meanwhile, I got busy as I sat in the control room, assessing the reports that had poured in from sources located in various parts of the city. I also reshuffled and repositioned the available force, keeping in mind the reports I was receiving.

However, around midnight, when I got a message requiring immediate attention, I had to put my juggling act on hold. The information I received on the wireless was that a crowd belonging to a particular community had gathered with aggressive intent outside a double-storeyed house in a sensitive area.

Accompanied by the additional superintendent of police (ASP), I rushed to the spot, where the station house officer (SHO), looking evidently out of depth, quickly summed up the situation for us. According to his version, the crowd belonging to the majority community had gathered at the chowk (square) and were alleging that a group of Muslims had collected in a room of the first floor of a building and were preparing to attack the Hindu mohalla. And it was further rumoured that the Muslim side was heavily armed. The SHO had tried to calm things down by asking the people not to believe in rumours.

But then an incident took place, adding fuel to fire. A gunshot allegedly aimed at a Hindu leader standing on the roof of his house situated diagonally opposite to the double-storyed building in question, was fired from the window of the room on the first floor.

The SHO said that he had somehow been able to contain the more belligerent elements among the crowd from throwing burning missiles with the intention of torching the room. I sensed that the restive crowd that had defied curfew orders was in no mood to heed dispersal orders. Flouting curfew is a serious offence and an unruly crowd can be forcibly dispersed even if it entails the loss of lives. However, rejecting the option of extreme measures, I decided to tackle Radhey Shyam, the Hindu leader, who had allegedly been shot at.

Radhey Shyam was a rabid communalist. He raved and ranted for a while until I calmed him down and asked how close this alleged bullet had come. He claimed that it was intended for his head and had he not bent down reflexively, there would be no Radhey Shyam talking to me right now. 'Are you sure?' I asked him.

'Sir, I distinctly heard the "ping" of the bullet passing close over my head.'

I glanced at the ASP and was reassured by his wink. Obviously, both of us didn't believe Radhey Shyam because we thought he had to be endowed with superhuman hearing ability to have heard the 'ping' of the bullet passing over his head.

It was well known that this man was on top of the Muslim community's hate list and he was well aware of this fact. Therefore, he knew that his claim of being shot at was plausible. The question to ask was: would he, in the face of the rumour that the inmates of the room were heavily armed, take the risk of openly exposing himself on his roof?

While I was pondering over all this, the ASP approached me and taking me aside said, 'Sir, the crowd is in an aggressive frame of mind. They are saying that when all is said and done, it was the other community that started it all. They are sore losers, since the wrestling match was won fair and square by the Hindu wrestler. And now this so-called attempt to assassinate Radhey Shyam needs a solid response, not only here but across the entire city. Since we do not have enough forces, I feel our first priority should be to persuade the leaders to placate the crowd.'

I saw his point but I said we had already tried that. 'It's time to call their bluff. I'll personally go up to the double-storeyed house and verify the allegation that a shot had been fired at Radhey Shyam by one of them.' When we told them of our plan, the Hindu mob's leaders, barring Radhey Shyam, agreed to wait, albeit reluctantly. It was a dangerous move for me to go into the 'lion's den', but it was Sunder Lal's example that inspired me to go up myself rather than send a junior officer.

The entrance to the room in the double-storeyed house, where the Muslim mob was supposedly holed up, was securely bolted from inside and in response to urgent knocks by the DSP, who I took along, a wary eye peeped through a crack. On repeated assurances, a youngster with a frightened expression opened the door. I recoiled at the appalling scene as a stale pungent smell assailed my nostrils.

The room was no more than a small cubicle, hardly big enough to contain two reasonably sized cots. Huddled together in it were about 20 men, women and children. Utter dread starkly visible in their eyes, they were sweating profusely, as much out of fear as being stacked like cattle in that small suffocating space.

A foul smell of urine and faeces pervaded the air. A small child aged about five, was lying on a soiled mattress and gasping in apparent discomfort. His name was Sajjad. A rusty 12-bore double-barrel gun reclined against the wall near the closed window that opened out onto the lane.

In immediate response to my questioning glance at the gun, Yaqub, who had opened the door and was also the spokesman, blurted out as if he was longing to unburden himself. 'Self-defence, Sahibji! We are all members of one extended family and when riots spread in the city, we all collected here in a bid to defend ourselves, realizing a little too late that we had made a mistake. This is the only dwelling that belongs to the minority community in this locality. We should have shifted to "safe" mohallas, but could not do so. The reason was that this morning we had all packed up to leave but Sajjad's condition became serious and we could neither move out nor do anything to get medical help.'

I looked at the five-year-old Sajjad who was clearly in bad shape and needed urgent medical attention. Yaqub continued, 'Somehow the crowd got wind of our presence here and collected in the chowk below, blocking our exit. They started shouting slogans, throwing stones and threatening to tear us apart.'

The DSP intervened and said, 'But what provoked you to fire through the window?'

He replied, looking at me pleadingly, 'Sir, it was I who fired but I did not aim at anyone in particular. Terribly scared at the sight of the unruly mob, I fired in the air, hoping to scare them away. I did realize at once that it was utterly foolish of me to have done that.'

I was convinced that Yaqub was telling the truth but I now had a big problem on my hands. The allegations of the Hindu leaders, I realized, were not baseless. Yaqub did fire the shot; it was only his unsubstantiated assertion that he fired in the air and not at anyone in particular. Even so, I assured the inmates that they need not panic and that the police would give them adequate protection. I then descended the stairs alone, after appropriately briefing the DSP.

A spine-chilling slogan invoking the local deity greeted me as I went down. Some of the leaders waved their arms in a gesture to calm the crowd and the bloodcurdling shrieks reluctantly subsided into an eerie silence.

The ASP met me at the bottom of the staircase and said that the requisitioned contingent had arrived and he had strategically and unobtrusively posted the men behind the crowd. He also said that he had a gut feeling that a fissure had developed in the leadership. 'If we manage to isolate Radhey Shyam, the rest of them are likely to go with us.'

Placing full faith in my experienced subordinate's assessment, I decided to tackle Radhey Shyam straightaway. I confronted him and said, 'You were not on the roof, Radhey Shyamji when the shot was fired. We were told this by witnesses who saw you mingling with the crowd below.'

Radhey Shyam shook his head vehemently and said, 'No sir, that is not correct. I was not down here with the crowd. You can ask them...' Some heads nodded to verify his assertion.

'What then is the truth? That you were in your bedroom when the shot was fired?'

Radhey Shyam blurted out in automatic response, 'Yes! I mean, no! I have already told ASP Sahib that I was on the roof.'

'As a matter of fact, you were talking to someone on the phone in the bedroom. We have reliable information...' This, of course, was a calculated bluff. We did have information but not confirmed as it wasn't from the person he was talking to but from one of this person's *chamchas* (hangers-on).

To finish him off, I landed the last punch. 'By the way, it was a shotgun that was fired. You well know it doesn't give out a single bullet and there is no "ping" sound like there is from a rifle or pistol!'

I noticed the amused response of the other leaders at Radhey Shyam's discomfiture. His immense unpopularity, even among the other Hindu leaders, was a well-known fact because of his tendency to always try to hog the limelight.

Leaving him squirming, I retreated to form the next strategy. After a hurried consultation with the ASP, I decided to wrest the initiative. Feeling that some exaggeration was required in my description of the mood in the double-storey house, I said to the crowd, 'Gentlemen, now let me start by telling you that the sizeable collection of people upstairs is a desperate and determined lot and they are heavily armed. It is true that the shot was fired but with the intention of scaring the gathering below and not to target anyone in particular. And, if this is not enough to make you think twice before doing anything rash, please look behind you—that should convince you that we, too, mean business.'

When the crowd turned to look back, they saw a cordon of armed policemen 'on the ready'. Ganesh Dutt, the sane element in the leadership, then came up with a request to permit him to speak to the assemblage.

His short speech ended with, 'We are law-abiding citizens. Let us disperse and let the law and order machinery take its own course.' It was well-timed, well-directed and correct advice by a seasoned leader who had sensed that the crowd, by and large, was looking for a way out and that resistance was futile.

As the crowd dispersed, I realized that that particular battle had been won but the war was still on. We had to make immediate arrangements for the little boy, Sajjad, to be taken to the hospital, and to shift the occupants of the room to a 'safe' locality. And we had to round up with all urgency the original mischief-makers: Feroze and Hafiz, who had gone underground.

The buck started rolling again, but I knew its halting place. I knew that sooner rather than later, it would come to roost on its favourite perch—my desk.

# 3

# Murder Most Foul

I stood on the third floor of my house in the early morning chill in a contemplative mood and looked out at the wheat field adjoining our compound wall. In the far distance was the Indira Gandhi Canal, which brought the water of the Bhakhra Dam to this part of the desert. It had transformed the area into a green oasis, no doubt, but it had also changed its culture forever. As the Ganganagar district in the state of Rajasthan shared a border with Punjab and Pakistan, it had always been a tough posting, and since the canal's advent, it had attracted many gold-diggers, making the crime rate soar. The police were always under pressure and the townsfolk had a love–hate relationship with it. Being a youngster and a newbie, I still had to prove my credibility and earn the respect of the Ganganagar gentry.

But all that was not what had got me into a reflective mood this morning. The question I was pondering was: How many more gruesome sights did those idyllic wheat fields hide? The haunting image, first narrated to me by the Sikhs, and then verified by my own eyes, kept flowing through my head. Last night, I was woken up by the sentry who informed me that two agitated Sikhs wanted to meet me urgently. They told me that they were farmers and shared a plot of agricultural land just adjacent to the house allotted to me, and that a mutilated, putrefied human torso was lying on their wheat field.

When I, along with the SHO, reached the spot to examine the scene, we found that marauding scavengers had savagely torn the body apart. Maggots had set in and a foul stench pervaded the vicinity. It indicated that the body must have been placed in the field some time back.

The face was blurred, yet there was no hiding whose body it was as the clothes obviously belonged to a boy. A puzzling clue was a pair of adult slippers lying in a clump of bushes a short distance away from the body.

As soon as the news reached the town, there was a violent outburst of emotion. A mob marched to the city police station headed by a person called Ram Lal. It took all the ingenuity of the police to control the mob fury. Ram Lal worked for Seth Ghanshyam Das, a reputable transporter with deep ancestral roots in the region, whose grandson had been kidnapped 10 days ago. Ram Lal, a tall, lanky and hollow-eyed man of 40 or thereabouts, spoke glibly and clearly had a gift for persuading people. He demanded justice on behalf of his employer and as an outraged citizen of a city where a 10-year-old boy could be kidnapped in the middle of the day in full view of the public. To top that, the police had not been able to find the boy for 13 days and now his mutilated body had been found instead. Ram Lal and the mob refused to be placated by our promise of swift police action. After all, he was justified in his refrain, which even I could not deny: 'Can the police action now bring the child back to life?'

We asked for a couple of days more to at least nab the culprits and bring justice and solace to the family of the boy. Finally, Ram Lal backed off with a derisive laugh as if mocking us and challenging us to do our best. I didn't feel confident of solving the case in two more days because most of our leads had gone cold but that was all the respite we had. Immense pressure came to bear on me not only from the public but also from my superiors. The media sensationalized the case further and the politicians could not be kept at bay for long. I was hardly a few months old in my posting as the SP of Ganganagar and I knew my reputation depended on this case.

The boy—Krishna—was the only child of separated parents and had been living at his maternal grandfather's house with his mother. The grandfather, Ghanshyam Das, a reputed businessman of the town, had taken them under his wing when the marriage between his daughter and her husband soured about five years earlier.

On the fateful day, Krishna as usual began walking back to his home after he was seen off by his schoolmates at the school gate, which was in the middle of the town bustling with activity at 11 a.m., and then never seen again. He disappeared without a trace. Seven days of intense search yielded no results.

On the eighth day, Ghanshyam Das gave me three letters—two written on inland forms, and one enclosed in a state government brown envelope. The two inland letters had been written in the Hindi script in a semi-literate hand; the other had Ghanshyam Das's address written in fine English letters on the brown envelope, but enclosed in it was another inland letter written in the same semi-literate writing in Hindi. The impression we gathered was that there were two persons involved in the crime—the writer of the three letters in Hindi and the person who wrote the address in English on the brown envelope. Evidently, a state government employee was somehow involved.

The writer's instructions to Ghanshyam Das were that on the next day he should board the fifth bogey from the engine of a particular local train going to Raisinghnagar, a town in the district of Ganganagar. He was told to carry Rs 10,000 in currency notes in a suitcase, and on reaching Raisinghnagar, he should leave the suitcase in the compartment itself and return to Ganganagar by the local train.

The kidnapper promised to safely return the child if the instructions were carried out and the police were kept out of the picture, failing which, he threatened dire consequences. Ghanshyam Das had rightly come to the police though in strict confidence. It had been decided that nothing would be lost in stage-managing the payment of ransom.

In accordance with the plan, Ghanshyam Das boarded the fifth bogey of the shuttle starting from Ganganagar at 8 p.m. carrying a suitcase stuffed with useless stationery. Plain-clothed police were placed at strategic points. As he was about to get down from the bogey at Raisinghnagar, a man came and sat next to him. He introduced himself as Bhatia, a businessman who was going beyond Raisinghnagar for a deal. On reaching Raisinghnagar, Ghanshyam Das requested Bhatia to look after the suitcase until he returned after meeting the station master. Bhatia waited for some time, then picked up the suitcase and got down. As he started moving away from the train, the police nabbed him.

However, after the interrogation, the trail turned cold. Bhatia claimed he was innocent and had got down with the suitcase to search for Ghanshyam Das to hand it over to him.

Ghanshyam Das received another letter on the eleventh day after the kidnapping. In it, the writer expressed his fury at him for seeking police help. We were flummoxed—how had he found out that Das had gone to the police? It was anyone's guess. Had he been watching the police apprehending Bhatia at Raisinghnagar? Or was there a mole in Das's house or, God forbid, within the police department itself? After all, in Ganganagar everything had a price.

The kidnapper gave Das another three days to pay up at a different venue, failing which the child would be killed. Ghanshyam Das was totally unnerved by this letter and was very keen to comply with the instructions despite assurances from us policemen that we were giving all possible attention to the matter and he should have faith in us.

We tried to reconstruct what could have happened, rationally considering each possibility. Our suspicion about how the kidnapper had got tipped off about Ghanshyam Das going to the police after the first letter became a kind of turning point in the case. We created a list of all Ghanshyam Das's far-flung relatives, friends and even acquaintances that he might have come into contact with in those first few days since his grandson went missing. In fact, we even had Ghanshyam Das on the list. The motive could still be ransom; he could stash away the ransom money and tell his debtors that he was unable pay them so that he could delay payments for a few more years. Except that when we checked, he didn't have any debts whatsoever.

In this way, we started ruling out people from our list after doing our investigations about their whereabouts. For instance, two of the child's close relatives had sustained staggering financial setbacks, and thus had a clear motive, but on following through, they didn't turn out to be very promising leads. The second letter narrowed down the suspect list even further, but we were still far from a final shortlist.

Then came the discovery of the body, giving a severe jolt to our calculations. The post-mortem could not ascertain the mode of killing but it did give a clue that the child had perhaps been killed within 10 or 15 days before the body was found. That gave us a chilling fact. The boy must have been murdered within a few days of his kidnapping, possibly even on the day itself. Then why were those ransom letters sent to Ghanshyam Das?

Cutting out all the white noise, we went back to what we were good at—deduction. On the basis of the clues available, the case was framed thus:

1. The child-lifter was perhaps well known to the child.
2. The motive was ransom.
3. There was a mole in Ghanshyam Das's house who was passing on information.
4. The crime was perhaps the handiwork of more than one person. If so, one of the suspects was semi-literate and only knew a bit of Hindi. The other suspect was in government service and could write in a fine English script.
5. The person asking for the ransom, the main brain behind the operation, had to know every move of Ghanshyam Das, including the fact that the first ransom bid had failed.

The fifth factor was a make or break question. When we asked Ghanshyam Das to recall what had happened as clearly as possible, he swore he had left the suitcase in the train and gone straight back home—he had told no one of his trip or its purpose. Then we asked him how he had he travelled back to Ganganagar. It was his answer that suddenly threw clarity, lighting up the occurrences in the case and pointing towards who the culprit was.

He said he had travelled back in a car. Our next question was: Who drove the car? And that's how we cracked the case!

The person who had driven the car was working as the *gumashta* (accounts keeper), employed by Seth Ghanshyam Das to keep all the accounts related to the trucks owned by Das. Though he had joined recently, the gift of the gab he was blessed with enabled him to inveigle himself into becoming very close to the family. On special occasions, he even drove the Seth around, especially on confidential missions. He was the one who maintained a logbook which contained rough accounts of payments made. A comparison of the handwriting in the ransom notes and the logbook yielded a breakthrough. The scripts tallied. Who was this treacherous insider?

To our utter surprise, it turned out to be none other than Ram Lal, the leader of the mob who had come with Ghanshyam Das in the delegation to the city police station the day before. The one who had spearheaded the protest with his rabble-rousing outcry: 'Can the police bring the child back to life?' Even then his impassioned leadership of the mob had been suspicious. Why was he so excited? What did he have to gain from making the police look bad? Where was he when the boy was taken?

We found out that Ram Lal had dropped out of college without a job in hand. However, he could live a comfortable life on the legacy left behind by his doting father though it did not take him much time to fritter away his small fortune on wine and women. Soon he incurred a huge debt. What he had going for him was that he was able to cleverly use his God-given charm to endear himself to people, winning their trust by his glib words. His way with words and false flattery had enabled him to get into the good books of Ghanshyam Das and his family after getting a job as an accounts keeper in the transport company the Seth owned.

We picked him up for questioning. At first he tried to lead us astray with his clever talk. But we were not as easy to impress as Ghanshyam Das had been. Under sustained interrogation, Ram Lal confessed that he had kidnapped the child. However, he insisted that he had no hand in the murder and that his two accomplices had committed the foul deed. These two were Shiv Shankar, a clerk in a government office, and Sewa Singh, the nephew of a Public Works Department (PWD) contractor.

Ram Lal confessed: 'About a week before the kidnapping, we three sat down for a drink at Shiv Shankar's den, a room that he had hired for such get-togethers. We needed money badly for our indulgences. We considered all sorts of ways and means. Then Sewa Singh, in a drunken state, suggested that the only way to get a good amount of money was to kidnap a rich person's child for ransom.'

Ram Lal told us that he, equally drunk, said, 'Let's do it.'

And thus was born the plot to kidnap the grandchild of Ghanshyam Das.

Ram Lal went on, 'One day when the child was returning from school, I met him and asked him to climb on to my cycle. He used to call me *Maama* (maternal uncle). When he asked me where we were going, I said that his mother was at her sister's house and I was to take him there. On the way, Sewa Singh trailed us on his cycle. When we reached Shiv Shankar's den, the boy looked perturbed as I told him that I had to meet a friend urgently after which we would proceed to his Mausi's (aunt's) house. On entering the place, the three of us overpowered the boy and tied him up. Then I wrote the first ransom note and posted it.'

Ram Lal told us that Shiv Shankar was tasked to give the boy regular meals, while both he and Sewa Singh were to take turns to keep watch on the boy and to check the boy's condition at intervals. 'That evening, however, Shiv Shankar came frantically searching for me and told me that the boy had died. We panicked and in the dead of night went and threw the body in a wheat field that was still unharvested.'

Then to create a misleading impact, Ram Lal wrote another letter on official stationery provided by Shiv

Shankar and enclosed it in a government envelope also given to him by the same person. He made Shiv Shankar write the address of Ghanshyam Das in English.

After the fiasco at Raisinghnagar, Ram Lal wrote another letter three days later. However, when the child's body was found, Ram Lal changed his strategy and led the protest to the police station.

But how had the child die? What had Shiv Shankar done? Or was it Sewa Singh who killed him? Was it an accident? Or murder? Ram Lal refused to say anything, and insisted he'd told us everything he knew. He wouldn't break down even under intense interrogation, flatly saying that the others would have to reveal what had happened as it was in their custody that the boy had died.

Meanwhile, we tackled the two other suspects. Sewa Singh looked bewildered and denied any hand in the murder. He accepted the fact that the three had imbibed drinks together about a week before the day of the kidnapping, but denied that he had suggested or had taken part in the diabolical venture.

Shiv Shankar proved more pliable. He was very nervous and readily admitted that he had participated in the plan and had supplied the envelope on which he wrote the address of Ghanshyam Das. But he maintained that he had nothing to do with the boy's murder. Intense, relentless grilling went on for some time and eventually we concluded that neither Sewa Singh nor Shiv Shankar had participated in the murder. Then Shiv Shankar said something very curious. He said he'd never set eyes on the boy in his life. Not even after the kidnapping. The boy was not confined in his den in the custody of the three friends. Then where was he? 'Ask Ram Lal,' was his frightened answer. It was clear he was telling the truth.

We realized that this case wasn't over yet. Even we were caught unawares by the sting in the tale.

We went back to Ram Lal and told him that his co-conspirators had confessed, but they said they never saw the child after the kidnapping. They had helped in writing the letters but had no idea where the child was held. So, we told Ram Lal firmly that it seemed he was the last person to see the child alive. Technically, the murder would be pinned on him. What did he have to say to that?

He was a tough nut—but he finally cracked.

His final confession went thus: 'After making the child sit on my cycle and telling him that I was taking him to his Mausi's house, where his mother was waiting for him, I suddenly changed course. Before getting him to the den, I told him that first we would chew some ganna (sugarcane). The child resisted and started crying. About 100 yards from the road, there was a thick cluster of unharvested sugarcane so I lifted the child down from the cycle and asked him to wait for me while I collected some sugarcane. The child was howling loudly by then. Somehow my nerves, already jangled by the kidnapping, suddenly screamed in irritation. I hadn't bargained for being a child's caretaker. All I needed was money and here the child was wailing so loudly—the noise was killing me. Unable to control myself I picked up a large stone and attacked the child with it. When he still wouldn't stop wailing, I strangled him.'

While running away from the scene in a panic, he told us that one of his rubber chappals gave way, so he left both the chappals behind in a clump of bushes. That proved to be the clincher, the 'nail in the coffin' to incriminate Ram Lal in the murder of Krishna, Ghanshyam Das's grandson.

The mourning for the child turned the hostility of the people to respect for the police. The local media reported the case extensively and I became a minor celebrity, though this phase didn't last long. Soon after, on my refusal to comply with a local politician's 'unethical' request, I was transferred out. I don't know if anyone else shed a tear at my departure, but Seth Ghanshyam Das and his family would surely have had moist eyes. The stint in Ganganagar gave me another motto to live by: 'Develop a thick skin when it comes to dealing with politicians and a thin skin for the public for whom we are selected to serve.'

# 4

# Grey Area

## The Bofors Case

### Prologue

Bofors boomed into prominence during the peak of the Rajiv Gandhi–V.P. Singh feud. Singh rode to victory in the general elections of 1989 on the plank of eradicating corruption in high places, and the Bofors deal was the flagship of his campaign. The matter of the purchase of this high-quality artillery gun from Sweden had deliberately been soft-pedalled by the ruling Congress government, and when the Opposition raised a mighty stink, the Congress had persuaded the CBI to treat it as a Foreign Exchange Regulation Act (FERA) infringement. It was alleged that certain secret amounts were deposited in Swiss banks by some intermediaries.

The CBI's request for a deeper probe was summarily shot down by the Swiss authorities on the grounds that depositing of foreign currency by aliens in their banks was not a criminal offence. However, the Opposition continued their tirade and became even more strident. On 16 June 1987, Rajiv Gandhi ordered a parliamentary probe when he was the Prime Minister. A Joint Parliamentary Committee (JPC) was formed under the chairmanship of B. Shankaranand (a minister in the Congress government) and consisted of members preponderantly from the ruling party. The members from the Opposition refused to cooperate and for all intents and purposes, the committee became a sham. After prolonged deliberations, it came to the conclusion that there was no exchange of tainted money in the deal. This was on 26 April 1988.

On 22 June 1988, *The Hindu* published documents indicative of Bofors having paid commissions to Indian agents. The series of articles was the result of a meticulously researched no-holds-barred effort by a journalist with impeccable credentials: Chitra Subramaniam.

The choice of Bofors (of Swedish make, a product of Nobel Industries) in preference to Sofma (a French product) was the decision in contention, as the latter gun had been placed at the top of the list in all the five evaluations that the Indian Army experts had undertaken during 1982–85. Rajiv Gandhi's meeting with Olof Palme, the then Swedish Prime Minister, in October, 1985 in Sweden, intriguingly coincided with the sixth evaluation.

All of a sudden, the experts discovered an enabling facet in Bofors which tipped the scales in its favour. It was the lightness and mobility of the gun, contended the evaluators, that gave it the quality of 'shoot and scoot'. Incidentally, General Sundarji who was Chief of Army Staff at the relevant juncture, admitted in a fortnightly magazine, on 1 September 1989 that he was in favour of cancelling the contract (with Bofors) but Rajiv Gandhi had shot it down.

On 15 November 1985, Bofors entered into agreement with a new agent, AE Services, a private firm which was promised a 3 per cent commission if the contract was signed before 31 March 1986—it was signed on 24 March 1986. The AE Services' account in Zurich was held by a non-existent beneficiary named Meiken. The most inexplicable facet of the Bofors saga is the fact that except for an Indian middleman, Win Chadha, the remaining beneficiaries of accounts held in Swiss banks were either non-existent frontmen of foreign vintage or agents/firms which had never negotiated arms deals.

The names released by the Federal Court of Switzerland, apart from Win Chadha and his relatives, included Ottavio Quattrocchi, an Italian businessman. The Hindujas floated three firms—Lotus, Tulip and Mont Blanc—with the sole purpose of receiving the alleged sleaze amounts in Swiss banks at Geneva. Quattrochi, the frontman for AE Services, was suspected to have been the main provider of the 'grease in the wheels' of the government's decision-making machinery, which finally came out in favour of Bofors.

When I took over as director, CBI, in the V.P. Singh government, naturally the Bofors case was at the top of my list, which I handled to the best of my ability. We managed to uncover the smoking gun (many of the deductions mentioned above were under my jurisdiction) but whose hand held it still remains unproven. This story is not exactly about the attempts at solving that case, but about my friend Bhawani Singh (name changed) from school, who got embroiled in the Bofors controversy and came to me for help.

Bhawani Singh and I were at Mayo College together for almost 10 years, and throughout were engaged in toppling each other from the position of the topper of our class, though in a surprisingly amicable and friendly manner.

As we were finishing school, both of us discussed plans for our future and together chose the first option that came our way: the Joint Services Wing (JSW) of the Defence Forces. Bhawani went for the army, while I opted for the air force. Due to a strange coincidence, both of us passed the written test, the interview and the physical tests, but failed the medical.

However, fate had other plans for me! My father was incensed when I told him about my intention to join the air force; he thought it too risky for his only child. I realized then that I had erred in not keeping him in the loop right from the start. Over the next week or so, I imagined myself in his shoes and empathized with his security concerns for me. There certainly was a danger involved and perhaps it outweighed the glamour of the job that had ruled my decision. Moreover, it had been the first option that presented itself; I had still to see what the rest of the world had to offer. I decided that continuing higher studies would be a better choice.

My father, perhaps, heaved a sigh of relief at my decision. In any case, he was extremely supportive of my wish to study as an undergradraduate for the BA Hons (Economics) course at St Stephen's College in Delhi.

Later I heard from mutual friends that Bhawani Singh, unlike me, had stuck to his guns, and after passing the medical test, had joined the JSW (Armed Wing). I never met him again until the day he came to my office in 1990 when I was the Director of the CBI.

By then, Bhawani had excelled in the army and reached the post of Lieutenant General of the Armoured Corps. It was about then, on 22 June 1988, that *The Hindu* had published documents alleging that Nobel Industries, a Swedish firm, had paid commissions to Indian and foreign agents for acting as middlemen to have the Indian army choose to purchase their product, the Bofors gun, over the competing French product, Sofma. Bolstering the suspicion was the fact that Sofma had been placed at the top in all the five evaluations that the Indian Army experts had undertaken during 1982–85, which was overturned in a sudden volte-face, alleged to be prompted by commission agents whose influence reached the highest levels of power.

One morning, not long after my taking over as the director, CBI, my personal assistant (PA) informed me on the intercom that Lieutenant General Bhawani Singh wanted to see me. I welcomed him with mixed feelings. What weighed against the pleasure of meeting an old and dear friend after a long gap was the reason for his visit. You see, it was Bhawani as a Lieutenant General of the Armoured Corps, who had spearheaded the team of army experts that had decided in favour of Bofors against Sofma.

As soon as he walked in, he gauged my expression and began hesitantly, 'Well, Shekhar...'

I interrupted him, saying, 'Look Bhawani, the CBI is known for giving a full opportunity to everyone to explain their conduct, even to a disreputable crook, before concluding in favour or against him. You are an old friend. I assure you that without clinching evidence, the CBI will not take a decision either way; that is, either to exonerate or to prosecute. I thought it was better to get this out of the way and tell you this straightaway.'

Bhawani smiled awkwardly. He didn't look very satisfied by what I thought was my generous offer of an opportunity for him to present his case. I asked him to sit down and ordered tea. So, what made him ill at ease despite my assurance? This needs further elaboration.

❧

I was posted as the Director General of Police (DGP), Rajasthan when Vinod Pande, the then Cabinet Secretary at the Centre, contacted me on the phone. He asked me whether I would like to join as director of the CBI. I accepted the offer and requested Hari Dev Joshi, the then CM of Rajasthan, to relieve me. The CM was kind enough to permit my deputation to the Centre for this posting. After joining as Director (incidentally on my third stint of deputation to the CBI), the Bofors case came up as a primary agenda.

My chief investigating officer, K. Madhavan, Joint Director, CBI, prepared an elaborate first information report (FIR) on the case and obtained my endorsement. Its worth was tested almost instantly in February 1990, when on our letters rogatory, the Swiss Court accepted our request and ordered the Swiss banks concerned to furnish details of the secret accounts held by the accused in our FIR. The entire country was agog with anticipation. Would the trail lead all the way up to Rajiv Gandhi, the leader of the ousted Congress Party? Who were the middlemen from the Swedish company and who were their Indian counterparts? Who had taken a commission to change the recommendation to Bofors?

The media and the public were following the Bofors case very closely, as V.P. Singh's credibility depended on it. The CBI was in the headlines of every paper and magazine in the country. The only news channel was the government-run Doordarshan in those days, so naturally, they carried our organization too. Though the matter had a distinctly political slant, I was determined to do my best to bring out the truth irrespective of what it revealed and how long it took. I kept reiterating in my interviews that while the acceptance of the letters rogatory by the Swiss was a great success, it would be a long-drawn-out battle because the case involved some foreign companies answerable only to the laws of their own country. We would have to continue dealing with the Swiss authorities to get results.

But even the initial success of the letters rogatory evidently rattled the ousted Opposition so much that it began a determined move to ensure Singh's ouster much before his term was over. Other fires he had lit were also coming back to singe him, particularly the acceptance of the Mandal Commission's report on caste reservations. The latter had disrupted the deeper identity-based character of the country and the students had erupted on the streets. All of a sudden, V.P. Singh, who was heading a shaky coalition, decided to step down. The Bofors case was far from solved but now what would be its fate?

Chandra Shekhar of the Janata Party replaced V.P. Singh as prime minister with the Congress Party's support. Chandra Shekhar's first call of duty was to make a courtesy call on Atal Bihari Vajpayee, a doyen of the Bharatiya Janata Party (BJP) and erstwhile Prime Minister (1998–2004). Chandra Shekhar bowed deferentially before Vajpayee, calling him his 'Guru'. Vajpayee is said to have smiled and said, *'Guru toh gud bane rahe, chela shakkar ban gaya'* (the Guru continues to be jaggery but the disciple has become as sweet as sugar). He was hinting at Chandra Shekhar's tilt towards the Congress Party.

Vajpayee had read the situation right as Chandra Shekhar provided the much needed relief to the Congress Party on the Bofors issue. He slowed down the Bofors investigation because his position depended entirely on the patronage of the Congress, whereas frustratingly so, the CBI couldn't carry on the case without *his* patronage. Since our investigation on Bofors was a government-to-government one, we couldn't proceed without the PM's support.

At that juncture, the CBI was poised to probe the role of AE Services which held the 'benami' account in a Zurich Swiss bank, with which Quattrocchi was connected. The contract for the purchase of the gun was suspected to have been sealed with Quattrochi's help. We, at the CBI, felt Quattrochi was the person who held the holster of the person whose hand held the smoking gun. It wasn't fair that the case could be stymied just by the change of government, but despite my pushing hard that exactly was what happened.

I knew my time as Director, CBI, was over. But where would my new posting be? Would I be accommodated in Delhi or would I have to return to my state as my punishment for not relenting on the Bofors case?

I was waiting for some shift in the status quo when the following story appeared in the *Hindustan Times* newspaper under the byline of its chief correspondent, V. Sharma.

**Shekhar** vs **Shekhar**

> Apart from Joshi (the then DIB), another officer whose removal in the recent police reshuffle has not been taken kindly is Rajendra Shekhar, a Rajasthan cadre IPS officer who was the Director of CBI. A competent man not known for hobnobbing with politicians, he, incidentally, is the only officer who hasn't been adjusted in Delhi in the recent round of transfers. One wonders what the Chandra Shekhar regime has against the PM's part-namesake who, despite having been made the CBI chief after V.P. Singh came to power, resisted all pressures by the previous Government in the controversial Syed Modi case. So much so that the mild mannered IPS officer even threatened to resign when asked to change the private counsel engaged for arguing the case on behalf of the CBI in the

Lucknow Session Court. It was for this reason that a general reason was issued for withdrawal of private counsel in all Government litigation. The counsel engaged for the Modi case, it may be recalled, were reinstated following publication of news reports which caused an uproar in Parliament.

Shekhar's conduct was professional not just in the Modi case. On several other occasions, insiders say, he bluntly refused to order investigations into complaints against Congress leaders. Only such cases where there was prima facie evidence were taken up during his tenure.

In the CBI circles it is well known that Shekhar wanted to stay in Delhi. He offered to quit the post he was holding after the fall of the Janata Dal Government with the request that he be accommodated somewhere at the Centre. But once the formal orders for his removal were issued, he insisted that he be reverted to his home state which, in any case, was in need of his services.

Shekhar was the Director General of Rajasthan Police before taking over as CBI chief. The short shrift he has been given only proves that it doesn't pay being upright and professional in a system dominated by sycophants and time-servers.

*India Today* published this article:

**Chandra Shekhar transfers two officials with impeccable reputations to Rajasthan**

Actions often speak louder than words. Prime Minister Chandra Shekhar's assurances that his government would not relent in pursuing the Bofors investigation as well as cases against big-shot economic offenders, began to ring hollow when the axe fell on two of the Government's most tenacious watchdogs in this area. CBI chief Rajendra Shekhar and revenue secretary Rajiv Lochan Mishra have both been given their marching orders—back to Rajasthan, their cadre state.

The development created a noticeable stir in bureaucratic and political circles because the two had been identified with a tough line on Bofors, erring industrialists, and the financial dealings of godman Chandraswamy.

But Chandra Shekhar is now using a unique explanation to justify their transfer. His aides are putting out the word that the move was in response to a request from Rajasthan Chief

> Minister Bhairon Singh Shekhawat who was insisting that officials with impeccable reputations be returned to his state to clean up his administration.
>
> Chandra Shekhar, his publicists say, will gladly transfer officials from the Centre to the states in the higher interest of fighting corruption at the state level.

Who knows what the truth really was, but when Bhairon Singh, the Chief Minister of Rajasthan, offered me a return to Rajasthan as DGP, I gladly accepted it. Though, I suspect that it was Bhairon Singh's camaraderie with Chandra Shekhar, rather than my efficiency as a cop that prompted Bhairon Singh to make that offer.

To come back to the point of Bhawani's presence in my office that morning, for obvious reasons it was an awkward situation. The strange look he gave me when I assured him that the CBI would be fair to him, in view of how fast I'd walked on the Bofors trail, wouldn't perhaps have sounded convincing.

That day Bhawani and I talked no more about the case. We exchanged pleasantries regarding the whereabouts of some of our old friends. After a while, he got up and said something like, 'I'll not tax your busy schedule further. It was nice meeting you after such a long time.' We both knew his overturning of the judgement of five past evaluations to favour the Bofors gun remained in the 'grey area'.

I felt that to come to a proper decision I would need a brainstorming session with my additional director, S.K. Datta, who was to become the director, CBI later. I always found him very wise and upright and, in this case, since Bhawani was my friend, Datta's impartiality and sagacity would be pivotal.

After considering all the pros and cons, we were back to square one: 'to do or not to do'? It was a grey area, we both felt, which meant we could neither exonerate nor prosecute Bhawani Singh.

The final call we took together was that in the circumstances, Lieutenant General Bhawani Singh had to be given the benefit of doubt.

# 5

# The Punjab Terrorists' Hit List

Even during the height of militancy, Ludhiana, a sprawling industrial city with a typical Punjabi ethos, seemed to be bustling with activity. The only indication of the unusual conditions was the proliferation of police pickets all over the city. This was in 1987, when terrorism in Punjab had attained its peak level.

Despite a palpable atmosphere of fear, or probably due to it, people had become mentally inured to the overwhelming police presence in the city, and went about their business as usual. That may have been the reason why the people of Ludhiana remained blissfully unaware of the country's biggest bank heist that took place in one of the busiest urban localities of Ludhiana.

On 12 February 1987, in a smooth operation lasting just about 45 minutes, a band of dacoits looted about

Rs 5.7 crore in hard cash from the vaults of the Industrial Area Branch of the Punjab National Bank. They then made a speedy getaway and vanished from the spot before the crime was discovered. It was a large sum of money but due to the public's exposure to so much crime news, not many eyebrows were raised.

Nonetheless, since it was the period when militancy was at the peak in Punjab, the case was thought to be sensitive enough to be handed over to the CBI for investigation. I was Joint Director of Special Operations and oversaw the case from the beginning. Over the months, we made several breakthroughs and as the supervisory officer, I had to make frequent visits to Ludhiana.

On one particular trip, there were reasons for us to rejoice. We had made a major breakthrough. The CBI had succeeded in identifying all the suspects in the case. Each of them was a member of the terrorist outfit—the Khalistan Commando Force (KCF), the best equipped and organized militant group of Sikhs in Punjab.

The list of suspects was headed by the self-styled Lieutenant General Sukhdev Singh, also known as Sukha Sipahi, who guided the KCF's field operations. His trusted accomplice, similarly self-styled as Brigadier Harjinder Singh, also known as Jinda, had already earned notoriety in the murder of General Vaidya (the retired Army Chief of Staff).

Though the entire lot of suspects had been identified in the Punjab National Bank dacoity case, they were still at large. Let me return to this particular Ludhiana trip after a significant diversion.

⁂

In March 1987, following a bloody shoot-out, the Delhi Police had managed to nab the elusive Jinda, who was adept at disguise. During the encounter with the Delhi Police, he was clean-shaven.

Since the CBI had a number of cases involving him as the major suspect, the Delhi Police handed him over to us. As he was seriously injured, we made arrangements with the Border Security Force (BSF) to keep him isolated in a well-guarded room of their high-security hospital complex on the outskirts of Delhi. When he had recovered enough to withstand rigorous grilling, CBI teams subjected him to intensive interrogation.

When the Deputy Inspector General (DIG) of the CBI was overseeing the matter, he came to my office to keep me updated with the latest developments. He spoke about the two self-declared objectives of Jinda's recent trip to Delhi and his disclosure was startling enough to make me sit up. I decided to visit the hospital myself.

As I entered the room, I heard a guttural sound of contentment. Jinda's grunt had, of course, nothing to do with my entry as I quietly sat in an obscure corner, out of his range of vision.

The reason for his upbeat mood was that the doctor had just informed him that he had recovered enough to be out of the 'critical zone'. His leg in plaster, hanging at a 45-degree angle, a grim reminder of the gory shoot-out with the Delhi Police, was in his reckoning a small price to pay for the 'cause' of the KCF, which was to create an independent Sikh state called Khalistan. He knew it was an occupational hazard of his high-risk lifestyle.

---

Jinda was a gregarious chatterbox and the CBI inspector, who was by training a good listener, had apparently struck a rapport with him. Jinda now addressed him in his typical Punjabi accent. Taking a crack at macabre humour, he said, 'Sahibji, Jinda is *jinda* (alive) today; as for tomorrow, he may be Jinda no more.' Evidently, he had a premonition that his days were numbered as most of his crimes attracted the death penalty. Like most desperate characters, he believed in life as it came, 'here and now without a tomorrow'.

The discernible finality to his life on earth with no reprieve in sight, evidently prompted him to launch into a confessional mode. He went on to relate his involvement in various crimes in Punjab and elsewhere, including Delhi. So when the inspector asked him to repeat the detailed reasons for this, his latest, visit to Delhi, he said in an almost casual manner that he, along with Satnam Singh Bawa, had come to kill Buta Singh, the home minister in the

Rajiv Gandhi government. He said this very casually, as if he had come to bid for Buta Singh at an auction. Jinda did not stop at that. He smiled mysteriously and said, 'And, of course, our visit to Delhi was also to complete the task that had remained unaccomplished at Ludhiana.'

To unravel the riddle behind Jinda's mysterious smile, let's go back a month to the Ludhiana trip where we had successfully identified all the suspects in the Punjab National Bank heist. I, as the joint director overseeing the investigation, was there to review the progress of the case. On the last day of this particular visit, I reached the bank's premises in the early hours to conduct an in-depth winding up session.

As my plane was to leave for Delhi in the late afternoon, we decided to have a quick brunch at the office itself. The Punjab Police's Deputy Superintendent (DSP), liaising with the CBI, sent a local sub-inspector (SI) dressed in plainclothes, to a well-known *dhaba* (roadside eating place) for some sandwiches and coffee.

The SI was on back-slapping terms with the manager. After they had exchanged loud greetings, the latter took him aside and pointed at a 'turbaned' Sikh (Sardar) and a clean-shaven person sitting together at a table close to the manager's desk. They were deep in an intense confabulation. The manager said in an urgent whisper that he could overhear snatches of their talk and was almost certain that they were terrorists discussing some dire future course of action.

As the SI glanced surreptitiously at the pair, he could not suppress a gasp of recognition. He realized that the Sardar, being who he was, was evidently trying to persuade his clean-shaven companion to undertake an urgent operation. Overhearing them, he could not suppress an audible gasp, excited by his discovery. Apparently, the sound alerted them and they hurriedly left the restaurant.

The SI rushed out after them but the duo had disappeared in a trice. He forgot all about the sandwiches and coffee and, climbing on his motorcycle, raced to the Punjab National Bank office. He went straight to the liaison officer, the DSP, and told him that he had just seen Sukha, the KCF chief, along with Jinda at the restaurant.

Initially, we CBI officers, felt inclined to brush off the SI's disclosure as a figment of his overwrought imagination. How could these 'most wanted' desperadoes openly move about; that too, when a CBI investigation involving them was in progress in that very town? But when the DSP vouched for his subordinate's expertise in identifying KCF terrorists, we were amazed at the gumption of these men! I asked the DIG, CBI, to ring up the local SP to request him to further follow up the lead, and to keep the CBI posted with the developments.

I boarded the plane that afternoon as scheduled. During the flight I thought about the daredevilry of the terrorists, but knew that such acts of needless bravado on the part of the terrorists, though rare, were not unheard of.

A month later, at the BSF hospital in Delhi, as I silently observed the interrogation of Jinda, I tried to decipher his enigmatic smile. His loaded comment about coming to Delhi to do another job pending execution (pun intended) instantly rang a bell—I recollected the episode at Ludhiana and felt that it had a direct connection with Jinda's mysterious mission (apart from killing Buta Singh, the home minister) in Delhi. It didn't take much for Jinda to reveal the entire story. He affirmed my assumption that the Ludhiana discussion in the restaurant was related to the Delhi mission.

Jinda told the inspector, 'We heard the policeman's gasp and turned around to look at him. Though he was not in "vardi" (uniform), we were convinced by his demeanour that he was a policeman, and when we saw his expression of recognition, we hurriedly left the place. At the dhaba, we were busy discussing a very serious development in the bank dacoity case. Our sources had informed us that the CBI was close to identifying all the suspects.'

Jinda continued, 'Sukha was extremely agitated by the news that the CBI was on the verge of naming the accused. He was not so bothered about himself being identified because he was already an accused in several cases but his main issue was that the money was now in jeopardy—the organization couldn't use their huge haul to buy much needed arms as anyone who tried to spend a large sum of money would be under intense suspicion. He strongly felt that *direct* action was the only way to derail the CBI investigation. And his version of direct action was to snuff the life out of any CBI officer directly connected with the investigation.' According to Jinda, Sukha was a great organizer but at times, very impulsive. 'That day he had called me to the restaurant to plan how to bump off the highest-ranking CBI officer in the city at the time.'

He continued, 'Sahibji, I was not for it at all. I'm a man of action myself, but I'm pragmatic too. I knew the CBI officer from Delhi was leaving that same night, and because we had no time and had not been prepared for action, the impracticability and futility of the scheme was obvious to me. So I was thinking of how to dissuade him by using his own tactic.

'Sukha is also called "Profitjee" in our close circle—because he always asks, before deciding on the course of action, '*Iss mein hamara kya profit hoga ji? Zara batayen.* (In what way would the KCF gain by the contemplated action? Please tell me.) But before I could elaborate on my plan to dissuade Sukha because of the impetuosity of his intent to kill such a high-profile target without preparation, the unexpected arrival and audible gasp of the sub-inspector effectively scotched his plan, at least for the moment.'

Nonetheless, Sukha had not given up on the original scheme of derailing the CBI investigation—when Sukha despatched Jinda to Delhi to attempt the attack on Buta Singh, he asked him to also explore the CBI angle.

Jinda, despite having his doubts, did contact his sources at Delhi, and as a preparatory move, asked them to monitor the movements of CBI personnel connected with the investigation and identify their residences, while he busied himself with trailing Buta Singh and his relatives. However, as a gratuitous side effect of the shoot-out leading to Jinda's arrest, the plan to eliminate CBI officials and Buta Singh was rendered null and void.

Jinda ended his engrossing narrative with a 'cluck of remorse', which reverberated for long in the North Block, even after the designated court had sentenced Jinda to death by hanging and even after the militant had been moved to a prison in Pune for his trial in the General Vaidya murder case. It was still echoing in its corridors when I returned to Delhi for my last stint as director of the CBI in 1990.

A 'cluck of remorse,' uttered by a dedicated terrorist to acknowledge failure, is a call to his accomplices to complete his unfinished task. I had the dubious honour of being on a hit list from which my name can never be erased. This is what my colleague M.K. Narayanan was reminding me about when he asked me not to walk alone from my CBI office in North Block to my residence in Tughlaq Crescent at twilight in the winter of 1990.

While I appreciated his advice, and even took it, it seems to me that as long as terrorism lasts, this terrorist 'TO-DO' list will just keep getting longer and longer. Why can't we find the political and executive resolve TO DO something about terrorism once and for all?

# 6

# Inside Out

## The Nirankari Baba Murder

### Prologue

The saying 'Home Sweet Home' signifies the comfort one feels after returning to one's safe zone after a long, tiring journey. For the Nirankari Baba, this saying was turned on its head.

There was an ongoing struggle between the Nirankaris and the Sikhs, as they, despite having faith in the same religion, differed in rituals of worship.

In 1978, on the day of Baisakhi, the annual Sikh festival to celebrate the founding of the Khalsa Panth by Guru Gobind Singh, their rivalry escalated into bitter discord. The Nirankari Mission had organized a *Manav Ekta Sammelan* (a function to advocate the unity of humanity) presided over by Nirankari Baba, the sect's spiritual leader, in a Punjab village. In a show of belligerence, the Kirtani Jatha, the fundamental religious group led by Sant Bhindranwale (yes, the very same of the 1984 Operation Blue Star fame), mounted a virulent attack on the Nirankari *samagam* (gathering). In the fight that followed, 13 Sikhs and five Nirankaris lost their lives. This incident was followed by some skirmishes, which culminated in a violent clash in Durg district of Madhya Pradesh on 19 March 1980, in which Nirankari Baba narrowly escaped bodily harm.

Following this incident, the Nirankari Baba's security personnel remained alert for a little while, but soon lapsed into the 'comfort zone' of the formalized routine of every day.

On 24 April 1980, the inevitable happened. At about 10.30 p.m., the Baba and his entourage came back to the 'safe' precincts of the Nirankari Bhawan in Delhi, after a *samagam*. As his car entered the Nirankari Bhawan and the Baba alighted from the front seat of the car, a gunshot was fired at him from the first floor. He collapsed on the spot, never to get up again.

It was a very sensitive case. The Nirankaris have a huge following both in Punjab and Delhi. Although the crime happened in Delhi, it came under the jurisdiction of the Punjab Police but was handed over immediately to the CBI by the Punjab government, run mostly by the Sikhs, to ward off any backlash by the sizeable Nirankari population in the state. This is the story of how the murder was planned and executed and how we finally caught up with the perpetrators and brought them to book.

The chairman of the Nirankari Mandal, Desraj Nirankari, was a well-known homeopath. Ranjit Singh, a Sikh who was an accomplished carpenter, visited Desraj one day, posing as a patient suffering from acute constipation.

This ruse was a strategic ploy to get inside the precincts of the Nirankari Bhawan. He was a glib talker and was soon able to get Desraj to accept him as a carpenter. Not only that, Ranjit managed to convince Desraj that he was an ardent follower of the Nirankari precepts and was very keen to join the sect. Ranjit Singh was aware that carpentry work was in progress at the *kothi* (the residence of the Baba), and since he had developed an amicable acquaintance with Desraj, he managed to convince him to recommend him as a carpenter. For the plan to be successful, it was essential for him to be employed at the *kothi.*

The chief carpenter at the *kothi,* Ram Singh, was not only impressed by Ranjit's work but also came under his spell. He permitted him to stay with the other carpenters on the first floor of the Bhawan. That was when Ranjit, in accordance with his plan, chose a small room that could barely accommodate one person.

Soon after, the Baba met his end on 24 April at 10.30 p.m., victim to a bullet fired from the first floor. Ranjit Singh vanished immediately after this incident, leaving behind a series of questions:

- ❖ Was Ranjit the one who fired the shot?
- ❖ Was the chief carpenter, Ram Singh, a collaborator?
- ❖ Who supplied the weapon and how did the gun reach Ranjit?

The CBI got its breakthrough when they subjected Charanjit Singh, an ardent Sikh devotee, to intense interrogation. He had been picked up along with many others in a routine raid of the quarters of fanatical Sikh devotees. Charanjit was an inhabitant of a colony across the Yamuna river. It turned out that he had readily accommodated in his house a five-member armed unit sent from Punjab and definitely knew about the main plan and that his five guests were sent as 'back-up' agents who would carry out another operation if the plot failed. Charanjit was a double agent of sorts. Even while being an ardent follower of Bhindranwale, he had managed to pose as a follower of the Nirankari sect and thus establish an intimate relationship with the working staff of the Nirankari Bhawan and keep track of the activities of the Baba.

During the investigation, Charanjit admitted that the back-up unit sent from Punjab had stayed at his house. However, following the success of the main plan, this team dumped their guns in the Yamuna and returned to Punjab.

To follow this lead further, it became necessary for the CBI to obtain the custody of Lakkha Singh, the leader of the back-up team. Aided by the Punjab Police we took in this elusive character for questioning.

'What was your role in the murder of the Nirankari Baba?' This was the tenth time we were interrogating Lakkha.

'I played no role.'

'We are aware that you were connected. Charanjit has already implicated you.' It was the first time that we confronted him with Charanjit's name, changing tack to surprise him with the name of his colleague. It was to let him know that we had Charanjit in our custody and he had told us whatever he knew. We had planned the interrogation in stages to break Lakkha psychologically. The revelation that a close colleague had snitched on him and that everything was unravelling was crucial to his break-down.

He protested, 'I was only the back-up. I didn't do anything. I don't know what else Charanjit is involved in but he harboured us in his house across the Yamuna.'

This was a major breakthrough. Now it made sense to let him stew in his own juice for the night and come up with the full dish next morning. So we left him sitting there for a long time, reflecting and contemplating. He expected us to come back to him later that day. But we didn't. It was important that he would not be able to sleep too well that night and left to mull over how much Charanjit had revealed.

The next day we began with: 'So were you the only back-up person?'

Sure enough, he was exhausted enough to stop stalling and give us information that would enable us to dive deeper into the case.

'No, there was Kabul Singh too.'

'What was his role?'

'He was a sharp-shooter attached with Ranjit Singh. He also brought along with him a gun to be used by Ranjit. Ranjit's prowess with the gun was very accurate and Kabul was only to finish off the job in case it was needed. The masterminds did not want Ranjit to be deprived of the "honourable" task of assassinating the Nirankari Baba. Not after all the effort he made to get into the Bhawan.'

Instead of going after the bait he had thrown regarding the 'masterminds' (which would probably lead nowhere because we knew he was only a foot soldier and the generals would have covered their tracks well), we decided to stick to the nuts and bolts of the killing.

'So, did Ranjit fire the fatal bullet?'

'You will have to ask him that. I wasn't there. He has certainly earned fame for it.'

'How did Kabul enter the premises?'

'The small room on the first floor was chosen by Ranjit because it could be exclusively used by one person only, and this room had a small window opening out into the lane at the back. Kabul climbed a rope thrown by Ranjit and entered through this window. After the shot was fired, both Ranjit and Kabul had escaped through this window.'

'How did they escape the *nakabandi* (the security measures)?'

'They had already entered Punjab before the local police's *nakabandi* was enforced.'

'And what about the back-up party?'

'Early next morning, I, as the leader of the back-up team, got the guns dumped in the Yamuna river and somehow managing to evade the *nakabandi*, I with my men escaped into Punjab through the outer periphery.'

His claim of dumping the guns in the river necessitated verification, so we took him there. He indicated the exact spot on the Yamuna Bridge from where the arms were thrown into the river. Charanjit had convinced the back-up team to choose that spot because the river ran deepest there. The CBI officers on the case decided that the recovery of the arms needed expert handling, so they requisitioned the services of divers from the Naval Headquarters based in Bombay (Mumbai).

Dressed in resplendent scuba-diving uniforms and impressive-looking equipment, they arrived with great aplomb and looked the very picture of effective competence. We felt assured that they would successfully scour the depths of the Yamuna and in a few attempts, would come up trumps with the jettisoned arms. However, after a whole day of diving, they had nothing to show for their efforts; they claimed that either the dumping spot was different or we had been misled. Their orders were to return the next day and so leaving us in the lurch, they went back to their base in Bombay.

I, as the DIG (Special Investigations), was the supervising officer and had to take the vital decision about whether to give up the search or persist with it. It was an awkward moment in the investigation because a lot depended on us finding the arms. I felt that Lakkha was not trying to mislead us and Charanjit, too, had corroborated his version.

Our dilemma was resolved by a suggestion from the local DSP, whose services had been lent to us by the district SP, on our request.

A bit hesitantly, he spoke up, 'Sir, why not make another attempt with the help of the local fishermen? They are expert divers too and have a good knowledge of the topography of the riverbed.'

Now, knowing that the nation's most adept divers had come a cropper, this suggestion, on the face of it, appeared bizarre. Nonetheless, we went with my hunch. We summoned the chief of the clan who was reluctant to undertake the task, but then his young son took up the challenge and persuaded his father and other divers to try to recover the arms.

To our utter surprise and elation, within a few hours, a hand holding a gun emerged out of the water's depths. Eventually, all the five weapons (highly sophisticated ones) were recovered. It was no less than a miracle, since even the nation's most knowledgeable, trained and fully equipped diving unit had failed to find them.

How did an unskilled, bare-bodied, undrilled rag-tag of a group come up trumps? We arrived at some interesting conclusions.

The first one was apparent. The naval unit had performed their task mechanically as compliance with an order, whereas the local divers did the job as a challenge with due dedication. The second was that there was a vital difference between the bottom of the sea and a riverbed; in addition, the stretch was located in the midst of an urban area, which meant that plenty of garbage muddied the water along with a lot of silting. The third factor, based on a principle and perhaps the most important one, was that the fishermen were locals and had grown up on the banks of the river, witnessing it when it ebbed or flowed in different stages. They knew that shifting silt was a natural phenomenon of a volatile river and hence it would be necessary to scour rather than skim the surface to reach the bottom of the riverbed.

In the next phase, the CBI decided to go after the masterminds behind the plot. It was necessary to subject Bhindranwale to intense interrogation. Since it was a highly sensitive issue, I, as DIG of the CBI in charge of this investigation, approached the director of the CBI, who nodded his assent but cautioned me to take due precautions.

I was well aware of Bhindranwale's penchant for talking only in Punjabi and so I had requisitioned the services of an SP well-versed in Punjabi to accompany me. Bhindranwale denied his involvement outright and fobbed off any attempts to pin anything on him. He was no Lakkha. He was used to talking to the police and was a pro at keeping them at bay. In any case, we didn't have him in our custody. After a few days, I realized the futility of persisting with the interrogation.

That was that and I decided to concentrate on the involvement of Ranjit and Kabul.

The CBI team was depending on the Punjab Police to arrest these two; a chargesheet had already been filed against them and others in the competent court. As it turned out, Kabul Singh posed no problem because he was killed in an encounter with the Punjab Police soon after. Unfortunately, we still didn't know who had fired the fatal bullet. The only person who could now tell us the truth was Ranjit Singh, but the local police was hesitant to lay hands on him because he had been appointed as the *jathedar* (leader of the clergy) of the Akal Takht as soon as he had reached the Golden Temple following the Nirankari Baba's murder! It was the Sikh community's way of honouring the killer of the leader of a turncoat sect that they had always wanted to teach a lesson.

Though the case was solved, I was left feeling unfulfilled because the main perpetrator, probably the man who fired the fatal bullet, was still at large. He was enjoying a charmed life of power and privilege for no good deed but for committing a crime. He was being directly honoured for murder!

## Epilogue

However, 15 years later, remorse or something close to it must have begun to ruin Ranjit Singh's sleep and he surrendered before the court on his own—he took the entire onus of the crime on himself. In his confession, he also emphatically affirmed that it was he who had fired the fatal shot.

# 7

# Pakistan Police's Poster Boy

On completion of our basic training at Mount Abu, seven of us as IPS probationers of the Rajasthan cadre, were posted with an army unit based on the Indo-Pak border. One of the main objectives of this attachment was to give us a 'virtual' feel of the Indian army's eyeball-to-eyeball confrontation with the enemy.

Our host battalion, the 4th Sikhs, was located at Mendhar in the Poonch–Rajouri sector opposite Pakistan-Occupied Kashmir (POK). As the duration of the attachment was only three weeks, the army was hard put to provide us with an encapsulated version of their life at the border. The experience that stayed with me from that training stint with the army was the night patrol.

We were woken up at midnight, without prior warning, and taken to a spot opposite Bhimber Gali,

Pakistan, for night patrolling on a rough dirt track. A sergeant major (SM) was detailed to put us through the drill.

Mendhar is on the pass between Poonch and Rajouri; though it's not very high, the border paths can be treacherous, especially after rain or snow. At the base camp, prior to starting for the track, we were briefed by the SM about the likely hazards involved in the venture. 'Sirs, due to unseasonal rains the path is slippery and narrow, so narrow that you can move only in single file. Please make sure that while you are on the move, your unwavering gaze is fixed on the back of the collar belonging to the Sahib ahead of you.' Then with studied nonchalance, he added, 'I must also mention that only two days ago, the Pakistanis had indulged in unprovoked firing, leading to retaliation from our side. Luckily, there were no casualties on either side. However...' He left the sentence hanging for us to fill in the blanks. Of course, we couldn't really guess what he was trying to hint at, but the danger involved in a night patrol sunk in, quickly making us shake off any drowsiness and stand ramrod straight.

He continued, 'I am carrying a torch to be used only in compelling circumstances. Fortunately, we have a moonlit night...*fir bhi, bade dhyan se kadam rakhen* (still, be very careful where you take a step). A large section of our patrol is in the forest where there will be no moonlight. And no talking please—kindly reserve your questions for later when the task is over. In case any of us gets lost, the password is "Collar". He paused again and enquired solicitously, 'Have I made myself clear?'

All of us, gingerly fingered our collars, and silently nodded.

❧

The forbidding terrain, the darkness, the eerie silence were discomfiting but despite that, like eager beavers we looked forward to the venture. As we were about to start, Rajpal (name changed) called out to the the SM, 'Hang on a minute. We need you to clarify something.'

Rajpal, the topper in our batch, was the most enthusiastic of us all, but he looked unsure for a change. His hesitation, curiously, was due to the one certainty he always had—his prerogative to lead us. But what had left him confused was SM's cautionary instruction to make sure each person had his 'unwavering gaze… fixed on the back of the collar belonging to the Sahib ahead.'

Rajpal asked, 'Whose collar should I fix my gaze on?'

'Mine.' The SM explained that he would be in the vanguard with his 'section' at the rear and we, the seven of us, would be sandwiched in between. We knew enough about outdoor drill to proceed strictly in accordance with the given instructions.

In the silence, the din of the jungle was deafening: a bullfrog's croak sounded like a human being strangled, and there was the ceaseless, strident chirp of the invisible cicadas beating on our nerves like tattoo-drums. The atmosphere was heavy with expectancy and all of us were keyed up in anticipation of our adventure.

Just then, two gunshots went off simultaneously! Stunned, we stopped in our tracks. The SM crisply asked us to lie facedown at once. We dived in unison as we heard the whine of bullets and impinging reverberations doing their rounds around and over us. I don't know how long we lay like that but there was time enough for us to pray to a significant number of the 33,000 Indian gods. To be caught in the crossfire of two warring armies when you belonged to neither of them seemed like a waste of a young police officer's life. Fortunately, Rajpal, too, kept his leadership tendencies in check and after a while, the shooting abated.

After a significant pause, the SM ordered a retreat in a crawling position. When he felt it was safe, he asked us to rise and walk back to the base. The project had to be abandoned.

Our feelings were a mix of relief and disappointment. The commanding officer (CO) of the 4th Sikhs, however, lifted our spirits with the announcement that he had found an even better alternative to the aborted night patrol drill that had almost led us into an eyeball-to-eyeball confrontation with the enemy.

To talk over the confrontation of the night, a 'flag meeting' had been fixed for a day later with the army's Pakistani counterparts. We were told that we would be part of the delegation. We exulted at this bonanza, though again we were in for another let-down! That evening, the CO informed us that despite the home ministry's *green signal*, the defence ministry had shown the *red flag* and rejected the proposal of a flag meeting altogether.

The CO elaborated, 'You may not know this, but for the first time, a dictator, General Ayub, has assumed power through a military coup in Pakistan.' It was October 1958 and it was quite a coincidence that this tumult in our neighbouring country had overlapped with our attachment to the army in the border sector. 'To strengthen his hold on the government, General Ayub is using the customary tactic of escalating tension on the border.'

For us it was a great disappointment—it was like offering to show us a much-hyped movie and then claiming at the last minute that the reels had not arrived.

All in all, I'd got a sneak preview of the border but was hankering for more after that stint with the 4th Sikhs as a probationer. Seven years later, in 1965 when I was posted as the SP of the Barmer district, I not only got to see the full movie but, in fact, a whole festival—it would be appropriate to say that I got more of the border than I'd ever bargained for.

In this story, I will narrate a lighter vignette of my border posting in Barmer, the main part of which involved very heavy work as it coincided with the India-Pakistan war.

A natural consequence of the Partition of India in 1947 had been the birth of cross-border crime or rather smuggling, its household name. To counter the growth of this crime, it became necessary to hold quarterly conferences between police officers of opposing sides, that is, of India and Pakistan. The SPs took turns at playing host on alternate occasions. During these meetings, discussions were held to control criminal incidents in a friendly atmosphere of give and take.

This done, recriminations, if any, were drowned in the sumptuous fare served by the host. The lack of liquor was made up by the spirit of bonhomie and further enhanced by the exchange of gifts, mostly inexpensive items like the fruit called 'keenu' from the Pakistani side and betel leaves from the Indians.

I began my posting as SP, Barmer, in June 1965 and my first border meeting was held, with Barmer playing the host, in the first week of August. The Pakistani delegation was led by the SP of Mirpur Khas, accompanied by the commandant (CO) of the Pakistan Rangers. As I greeted my counterpart SP from across the border, and he was about to introduce me to the CO of the Pakistan Rangers, I gaped in astonishment.

This person, sporting a thick crop of wavy hair, a ruddy complexion and green eyes, was exceptionally tall and strikingly handsome. A bit of rotundity only enhanced his stature. But what had evoked my surprised response was not his appearance. I knew the man!

Before the SP, Mirpur, could name the CO, I asked him myself, 'Mr Fazal Mahmood, if I am not mistaken?' Taken aback, the Pakistani officer smiled shyly and said '*Jee janaab, aap mujhe kaise jaante hain* ('Yes sir, how do you know me)?'

'I've met you before,' I blurted out. He frowned trying to figure out where we had met.

Even before I'd first met him, I'd idolized him as a sporting idol in my youth. He was the first cricketing hero of Pakistan and it was his bowling prowess that was praised by Neil Harvey, the famous Australian opening batsman, when he said, 'Fazal can make the ball talk…'

Fazal's most devastating performance ever was at the Oval in 1954, when he bowled out the England team twice, taking 12 wickets in the match. A British newspaper mourned the fact with the headlines, 'England *Fazalled* out'.

During his cricketing career, Fazal made full use of his height and long arm to become one of the most effective medium-fast bowlers of his time. He was selected to represent India in 1947 at the time when the Partition was just round the corner. In the event, he opted for Pakistan and joined the Pakistan Police as an inspector. For the next 15 years or so, that is, before he retired from the cricketing scene in 1962, his job in the police force remained a sinecure one as he pursued his Test cricket career assiduously. Nevertheless, he earned many promotions and just rewards in appreciation of his exploits in the sport.

When I had met him all those years ago, it had been a momentous event of what I thought was my budding career as a fast bowler. However, I now decided that as the convenor of the meeting of the Indian and Pakistani delegations, business came first. That was the reason why I said I would tell him about our first meeting after our conference, at lunch. 'I want to tell you about it in a leisurely way, rather than say it abruptly now, as I have always savoured the memory.' In response, he gave me the famous Fazal dazzling smile, a smile that women would swoon over during his heyday. I could see that it still packed quite a punch.

Usually, these conferences about smuggling were mostly routine since the cases were minor cases of cattle thefts and offences like trespass. But this time it was different. I had a very pressing matter to discuss with my Pakistani counterparts.

A very serious incident involving criminals from across the border had taken place in our district about a week earlier, perhaps the biggest dacoity since the Partition. At a border village near a subdivision called Chohtan, the dacoits had tied up the village *baniya* (trader), who was known for amassing wealth through usury, and looted huge amounts of cash, jewellery, gold and silver ingots. They'd cleaned out his entire treasure hoarded over several decades. Then they had escaped on the family's pedigreed horse and their own camels, after firing a few rounds to scare off the local villagers.

The deputy superintendent of police (DSP) of the Chohtan subdivision, a seasoned officer, marshalled his troops, including a *khoji* (an expert tracker) to identify hoof marks and informed me that he was going after them. I told him to wait for me as I felt we needed more than just his small posse to go after such brazen dacoits. By the time I reached the spot with reinforcements, already about an hour or two had elapsed.

However, we gamely gave chase. What made the task simpler was the fact that for the khoji, the horse's distinctive hoof prints were easy to make out. Our balloon-tyre 'jeeps' were as adept as—if not more—than the dacoits' camels in tackling the sand dunes. Another factor that worked to our advantage, which we discovered only later, was the uncooperative attitude of the horse.

The pursuit matched the best screen chase one can imagine, but unfortunately, the ending wasn't in our favour. The dacoits crossed over the porous border barely 15 minutes before we could catch up. All wasn't lost though. On our side of the border, panting in loud snorts and perspiring profusely, stamping its feet and neighing in annoyance, stood the thoroughbred horse with its 'load' intact. It had obviously been abandoned because of its recalcitrance; its sweating flanks reinforced our belief that we had missed the dacoits by a whisker. The hurried change in their strategy, forced by our close pursuit, must also have forced them to leave most of the loot behind.

We suspected the dacoits belonged to the notorious gang of Chhachro, a sprawling hamlet in Mirpur Khas. I had expected my counterpart not to cooperate in handing over the dacoits, and as it turned out, he *did* hesitate. After all, to admit that Pakistani nationals had crossed over the sovereign borders of India, a border bristling with animosity between the neighbours, would not go down well on his record. That, too, when his senior officer was present. He looked across at Fazal Mahmood, the CO of the Pakistan Rangers.

His boss surprised both of us. He said, 'We got information regarding this heinous deed a few days ago. We are on their tail, not to worry, Shekhar. I can assure you that we will nab them. We hope to give you the good news much before our next meeting at Mirpur Khas.'

The SP looked relieved that the CO had taken up the delicate matter. But I, more than him, felt I had a reprieve. I had been dreading a long-drawn-out discussion and negotiations to get the Pakistanis to look into the matter. But in a jiffy, Fazal Mahmood had not only promised they would go after the criminals but affirmed that he was confident of apprehending them soon. The hero of my youth had given his word that the dacoits would be caught within the next month. I thanked him profusely for his support and then we raced through the other minor matters that required mutual cooperation.

At lunch, I told him where I'd met him. Fazal Mahmood had his Test debut in 1952 for Pakistan in the first Test at Delhi. I was a college student at Delhi, a frail fresher with a bloated ambition as I yearned to play for my college, and beyond, even for my country, as a fast bowler. All of us aspiring cricketers were mesmerized by Fazal, not only because of his devastating speed but also for his striking looks. That winter, when Fazal became perhaps the first Pakistani cricketer to endorse an Indian brand of hair cream, most of us budding cricketers switched to that particular pomade in the hope that his association with it would work magic on us too. Alas! I can only say by personal experience that all it gave me was a greasy, gooey hairdo!

Unlike me, he was extremely popular with young Indian women, specially at Delhi University, which included Miranda House College, my future wife, Shiela's, alma mater. This created an intractable problem in that access to him by the male admirers was squarely blocked by a ring of female fans who forever surrounded him wherever he went. If they had their way, they would have followed him into the field as well.

Then we got lucky. In our time, Tests were spread over a period of six days, Sunday being an off day. On that particular Sunday, our coach persuaded Fazal to come to the university ground and give some tips to young aspirants. Since Fazal's ball did the talking, he wasted no time and got into action straightaway.

His run-up was fluid grace in motion, his delivery smooth and razor-sharp. Famously known as the 'Swing King', he was deceptive like an eagle stealthily swooping over its prey. He was a *total* package.

He broke the spell to explain how to use the ball's seam for swing bowling, a practice the Pakistanis have continued to hone to perfection. He then watched us bowl and was impartial in his praise. All he said in each case was 'Great.' This one word, despite its lack of comparative evaluation, was still 'great' for each one of us.

When the coach was introducing us to him individually, Fazal looked at me critically and repeated, 'Great. You must eat more eggs though.' He was alluding to my lean frame and I, despite being a total vegetarian, took his advice seriously and had a vigorous go at all sorts of egg preparations from then on. In fact, I still try to eat an egg every day for breakfast.

---

I reminded Fazal about his visit to the university playground in 1952, during his Test debut for Pakistan against India. I said with fervour, 'And what a great honour it was for us aspiring cricketers to see you perform magic with the new ball.'

He smiled modestly and said, 'Ah! That was *great*. It was *great* meeting you and everyone else.' I don't think he had the foggiest recollection of the incident but the word 'great' was as significant for me now as it had been then and I took it in 'great'fully with my heart and soul.

It was time to say goodbye and as we warmly shook hands, the SP of Mirpur Khas, the designated host of the next meeting, declared, *'Insha'allah, phir milenge'* (God willing, we shall meet again). And I responded with a warm handshake. 'If we do, I hope there'll be good news that the dacoits are nabbed.'

---

However, the spoilsport Ayub Khan intervened and declared war against India in April, 1965. The Chhachro gang would, presumably, have rejoiced at Ayub's declaration since the Pakistan Rangers got embroiled in the war effort. Fazal Mahmood wasn't able to bowl out the Opposition this time, as promised, but it was in the circumstances inevitable.

**Postscript:** When Fazal was charming the young women of Delhi University, I was wooing Shiela, my future wife. I met her after Fazal had endorsed my bowling as 'Great' at the nets and told her excitedly: 'Yesterday I met Fazal Mahmood!' She looked bemused.

I was amazed at her lukewarm response and asked, 'You have heard of him, haven't you?'

Her indignant 'Of course!' delivered a stab of jealousy right into my heart.

'So I presume like all Mirandians, Fazal Mahmood has bowled you over too?'

She gave me a confused look, 'He's not that good-looking.'

I was puzzled, thinking that she must be the first human on earth who had been so unenthusiastic about the looks of the wavy-haired, square-jawed, blue-eyed, athletic sportsman, Fazal Mahmood.

She continued, 'You are talking about that Bollywood singer and actor? The one who acted in *Aaram* recently with Madhubala and Dev Anand?'

'That's Talat Mahmood!' I burst out laughing with relief. Earlier, her lack of interest in cricket had troubled me but that day, I was thankful that her ignorance had made her miss being swept away by the phenomena called Fazal Mahmood.

# 8

# A Novel Murder

## The General Vaidya Case

### Part I

### Prologue

'A compulsive page-turner,' claims the blurb on the cover jacket of the explosive mega-thriller, *Triple*, a Ken Follet novel. The book's theme revolves around the mysterious disappearance of a uranium ore shipment weighing 200 tons, large enough to build 30 nuclear weapons. However, the theme in itself is not particularly relevant to the following narrative, but the manner in which the book was put to use.

A diehard Follet fan, it seems, took the blurb at its word and carried the paperback edition along with him even though he was on a serious mission that required focused reconnoitring on the streets of Pune. It is a matter of conjecture whether he found time to finish reading the book. The confirmed fact, however, is that he used the book's last page to jot down the registration number of a car—DIB 1437. And this unwitting act provided the CBI with a vital clue in one of the most sensational murder cases it has investigated.

In an oblique way, the government was responsible for this murder, too. In a bid to neutralize the Nirankari faction, the Congress government had given undue prominence to Damdami Taksal's leader Jarnail Singh Bhindranwale, in the build-up to Operation Blue Star. At first a mere preacher, he was given significance as a Sant (religious leader) by the government who meant to use him as a challenge to the Akali leadership that was powerful in Punjab. But by now it's well known and well documented how this move misfired badly. The government had let the genie out of the bottle. Consequently, Bhindranwale upped the ante and began clamouring stridently for a separate state called Khalistan and rapidly expanded his activities beyond Punjab.

Indira Gandhi, after much deliberation, decided to give in to the hawks who were advocating swift army action to flush out the terrorists from Amritsar's Golden Temple complex, unarguably the most revered symbol of the Sikh faith.

The three Generals spearheading the army action—Operation Blue Star—were the Commander-in-Chief,

General Arun Kumar Vaidya, his deputy, Lieutenant General Sundarji, who was intricately involved with planning and execution, and Major General K.S. Brar, the 'man on the spot' directing the operation. During the entire episode, General Vaidya, assuming a low profile, remotely controlled the action, whereas the other two Generals were constantly in the limelight. Not that keeping a low profile saved General Vaidya's life. The terrorists got him first, in fact.

Despite meticulous preparations and awesome firepower at its command, the army's action turned out to be a messy affair. Operation Blue Star was launched on 5 June1984 at 10.30 p.m. The army had not bargained for such a stiff opposition. In particular, they had to contend with stiff resistance from Sant Bhindranwale's followers who had barricaded themselves in the hallowed precincts of the Akal Takht, the spiritual sanctum sanctorum of Sikhism.

The Sant's devotees were equipped with modern, sophisticated weaponry, which they were capable of handling adroitly, thanks to unstinting 'foreign' help in providing them with arms and training.

Acknowledging grudgingly the strategic edge that the terrorists had, General Brar had commented, 'The militants' automatic weapons were so well suited to cover the Akal Takht quadrangle that they could continue with their devastating fire, our tanks notwithstanding.'

As a consequence of this unexpected resistance, there were heavy casualties during the army action. The Indian government's 'White Paper' gave out the figures of 4,712 persons killed and 10,000 arrested. Bhindranwale perished in the intense battle too.

The trail of hatred and vengeance in the wake of Operation Blue Star would culminate in the assassination of Indira Gandhi on 31 October 1984, just six days following Diwali, the festival of lights and rejoicing. This was followed by ruthless retaliation at Delhi and other places against innocent Sikhs, a mindless massacre of Sikh lives and desecration of their gurdwaras, further complicating an already complex situation.

Soon to be caught in the vicious cycle of retribution would be Indira Gandhi's top generals. This story outlines the fate of one of them, the Chief of Army Staff, one of the officers responsible for Operation Blue Star—General A.K. Vaidya.

General Arun Kumar Vaidya, on his retirement, decided to shift back to his hometown, Pune. Without frills and fanfare, he joined the ranks of 'retired' officers, hoping to enjoy a quiet, tension-free life far removed from the charged atmosphere of Delhi. There was just one major setback to his decision. The intense security-conscious ambience of the Indian capital was lacking in Pune, and its absence would largely enhance his vulnerability. Imperceptibly but definitively, he became a victim of neglect by the state as after a decent interval, his personal security was scaled down. Head constables, each on 12-hourly shifts, were deputed to guard him, but this arrangement amounted to nothing more than a token recognition of his vulnerability.

---

At 9 a.m on 10 August 1986, Head Constable (HC) Ramchandra Baburao Kshirsagar reported for his duty as the personal security officer (PSO) at General Vaidya's residence located at 47, Koregaon Park. He relieved H.C. Thorat, the PSO on night duty, who had 'nothing to report', implying that things were normal. The day duty PSO was required to accompany the 'Sahib' and 'Madam' on their outdoor chores, which mainly comprised shopping for daily domestic needs. General Vaidya, well aware of the lurking threat to his life, took whatever precautions he could. One of these was to invariably inspect the outer periphery of his house before venturing out. Accordingly, on 10 August 1986, at about 10.30 a.m., he emerged from the interior, took a careful recce of his house and then went back inside.

At 10.45, accompanied by his wife, he came out and Mrs Vaidya sat next to him. The PSO, armed with a loaded revolver and 30 spare bullets, sat directly behind Mrs Vaidya. Since the retired general was more likely to be the target of a terrorist attack, it was under his orders that the PSO occupied the seat behind Mrs Vaidya with a view to widen his arc of vision on the 'vulnerable' side, namely, on Vaidya's right flank. As soon as the seating arrangements were satisfactorily sorted out, Vaidya drove the car out of his front gate.

Meanwhile, a pair of Khalistan Commando Force militants, disguised as Hindus, with their hair cut short, had meticulously planned on disrupting the Vaidyas' routine shopping trip.

Sukhminder Singh, also known as Sukhi, arrived at Bombay under the assumed name and identity of Ravinder Sharma. He hired 307, Om Apartments, Borivali for his purported dealings as a small entrepreneur. Then, between 21 January and the end of February 1986, posing as the owner of a plastic industry at Borivali, he contacted various property dealers in Pune and evinced keenness to expand business and build up another base at Pune. In pursuance of this avowed purpose, he along with Baljinder, also known as Raju, hired a flat in Salunke Vihar, Pune, thus completing phase I of the plan.

Sukhi was only the architect of the plan, not the executor. It was at this point that it was over to Harjinder Singh Jinda, the very terrorist we have encountered numerous times earlier in my accounts.

**Part II**

Head Constable Kshirsagar, the security guard of General Vaidya, was a member of the Armed Police (AP) and had been serving in the city for 22 years. During the last four years, he was attached to the police commissioner's office as a gunman, and this fact perhaps was the deciding factor in his posting as the General's PSO. Kshirsagar was the main eyewitness in the case and his version of the tragic events that unfolded, as narrated to the CBI, went something like this:

'Sahib drove the car via the Food Corporation of India's godown and over the railway overbridge. He came onto the Koregaon Park and Circuit House crossing and negotiating turns, he passed in front of Southern Command and Capital Cinema, and then stopped at the Naaz Bakery. At that point, Mrs Vaidya alighted and after buying some food items, returned to the car.

'The journey began again and after criss-crossing various roads and turnings, General Vaidya halted the car at Shivaji Market and Madam got down to buy vegetables. I helped her cross the road, returned to the car and stood alongside General Sahib's door till she came back in about 15 to 20 minutes after making her last purchase from Hotel Dorabji.'

On the return journey, he said, the car had a smooth run through Taboot Street up to the Cafe

Naaz crossing, turned right on Tarapore Road onto the Southern Command crossing. And, just as the car reached the Queen's Garden crossing, a cycle-rickshaw came from the opposite direction, forcing the General to slow down the vehicle. Instinctively, the PSO, who was sitting behind Mrs Vaidya, looked back over his left shoulder, swivelled and stretched his right arm from the rear window to direct the traffic coming from behind.

Kshirsagar's reflexive arm movement was obviously not a well chosen one since it literally involved turning his back to the specific task allotted to him—to be on the lookout for dubious activity on the vulnerable side of the car, that is, towards the right flank.

As the car came onto the crossing of Queen's Road and Abhimanyu Road, a black motorcycle suddenly appeared on the car's right flank and cruised along. A clean-shaven youth was on the driver's seat with another turbaned and bearded person riding pillion. In a matter of seconds, the driver expertly manoeuvred the bike so as to give the pillion-rider a clear, wide-angled view of his target. The assassin aimed and fired a volley of three bullets from a .32-bore pistol.

General Vaidya was hit on his head from close range and collapsed sideways on to Mrs Vaidya's lap as streaks of blood began oozing out of his wounds. The car careened dangerously to the right and dashed into a cyclist who jumped off and escaped with minor bruises.

The PSO was stunned into inaction by the sudden turn of events, even allowing the motorcyclist to take a U-turn and speed off from the scene of action.

Though one bullet had grazed her body, Mrs Vaidya cradled her husband on her lap and disregarding her injury, repeatedly urged the PSO, 'Stop a car! Stop a car!' Finally, the driver of a Matador van stopped in response to Mrs Vaidya's desperate pleas, but it was too late. It could only carry General Vaidya's dead body to the Southern Command Hospital.

Almost a month later, Sukha, the pillion rider who had fired the fatal shot along with an accomplice, visited Pune on 7 September 1986. They had to do so to collect the murder weapon that had been left behind in the hired flat at Salunke Vihar.

Then in a fateful twist, came the denouement, proving that meticulous planning and utmost precaution are of little use in the face of providence.

On the return journey, the motorcycle met with an accident at Pimpri, a locality in Pune. The local police rounded them up for interrogation and when the registration number was routinely tallied with of the motorcycle in the relevant police records, they made a stunning discovery. It was the vehicle that had been used in the Vaidya murder. It was an almost unimaginable breakthrough. The police had netted the vehicle used in the murder, the murder weapon and the chief assassin (Sukha), all in one fell swoop!

But the onus lay on the police on how to pin down the evidence that all these were clearly used for killing General A.K. Vaidya. Here comes the clincher. It was Ken Follet who came to the rescue of the CBI. The search of the flat in Salunke Vihar revealed the book, *Triple* by Ken Follet. And in that book they found the clinching proof they needed—right there on the last page was the number DIB 1437 written in pencil. It was, of course, the number of General Vaidya's Maruti 800 car, the vehicle driven by the General on the fateful day. While casing out the General's house and habits, the assassin, an avid Ken Follet reader, had noted the General's car number casually at the back of the book. That unwitting step became the key evidence linking the whole chain of events and the KCF's involvement in the murder. The interrogation turned sharply from there on and Sukha was forced to reveal all the details.

The CBI was able to establish beyond doubt the identity of both the assassins, as also the fact that the vehicle used by the assassins was the Ind Suzuki motorcycle—MFK-7548. Sukha was lodged in a Pune prison and a red alert was put out for Jinda, who had driven the motorcycle with Sukha as the pillion rider.

As described in an earlier story, Jinda was later caught after the bloody shootout with the Delhi Police in March, 1987. The CBI had interrogated him regarding his involvement in various terrorist incidents perpetrated by the KCF, including the Vaidya murder; and subsequently, he was transferred to Yerwada Jail (Pune) to join his partner in crime, Sukha.

## Epilogue

The CBI filed the chargesheet in the court of the Special Judge designated for CBI cases on 14 August 1987. Due to security considerations, the trial was held in the jail premises itself. The court pronounced its judgement on 21 September 1989 and sentenced both Jinda and Sukha to capital punishment.

Jinda and Sukha were 'hanged till dead' on 9 October 1992.

**Clarificatory Note:** I have neither supervised the investigation nor overseen the prosecution of this case, but have included this case as it is eminently representative of the CBI's investigative temper and is one of the most dramatic and challenging cases ever investigated by it.

I have had three separate stints with the CBI, totalling approximately 14 years, and each moment spent with the agency has been part of a rich learning experience. It is my way of paying tribute to the organization.

# 9

# Justice Delayed Is Still Just

## The L.N. Mishra Murder Case

On 2 January 1975, L.N. Mishra, minister of railways in Indira Gandhi's cabinet, arrived on the platform of Samastipur (Bihar), to inaugurate a newly-constructed broad-gauge line between Samastipur and Muzaffarpur. After completing his speech, he turned to climb down from the dais. In a split second, a thunderous sound stunned everyone present. It was a bomb explosion, and as the smoke began to clear, Mishra was found lying there, seriously injured. He was transported for treatment to the Danapur Railway Hospital, but passed away the very next day.

The case registered by the state police was transferred to the CBI on 7 January 1975. This decision did not go well with the local police as L.N. Mishra was a Bihari and his younger brother,

Jagannath Mishra, was a top political figure of Bihar. Moreover, the local police had their own version of the incident in which they suspected the hand of three local miscreants.

The CBI, who did a thorough job, concluded that Santoshanand 'Avdhoot', a member of the Anand Marga, a global organization that called itself 'spiritual' and dedicated to social service, and eight other Anand Margis were guilty of the crime, and filed a chargesheet against them. It was averred in the chargesheet that the headquarters of the Anand Marg were in Bihar, and these members had decided to eliminate L.N. Mishra because he wielded a lot of clout as Indira Gandhi's close associate and the Bihar government functioned under his diktat.

The Margis firmly believed that Mishra was determined to completely neutralize their influence. Their founder, 'Anand Murti', was already in jail and they strongly believed that Mishra had been instrumental in ensuring that he did go behind bars.

When the Janata government came into power in 1977, the case acquired a political twist and a fresh look in the matter was ordered. The angle taken by the Janata government was that Mishra was privy to many embarrassing secrets and the central government itself, at the behest of Indira Gandhi, decided to eliminate him with the support of the local member of the legislative assembly (MLA), who tasked three local petty criminals for the purpose. This was the state police version right from the start.

I was then a junior deputy inspector general (DIG), and entrusted with the job of verifying the facts of the case more than a year and a half after the chargesheet had been filed. After my investigation, I submitted my report, stating that the local police version was baseless, and mentioned in passing that the CBI had done a thorough job in nailing the real culprits.

Expectedly, my report was not well received by the ruling dispensation; more so, as their stance was bolstered by the Public Union for Civil Liberties (PUCL) a well-known human rights watchdog. C.V. Narasimhan, Director of the CBI, was convinced about the authenticity of my report but was hamstrung by the contradictory stance of the political bosses. He was summoned by Chaudhary Charan Singh, the then home minister in the Janata government. The director was a Tamilian not at all well versed in Hindi, whereas Charan Singh had a penchant for that language.

C.V. Narasimhan, therefore, asked me to meet the Home Minister to explain the CBI viewpoint. Now, considering my 'raw status' and lack of experience in treading the corridors of power, I was not exactly looking forward to the prospect of appearing before the second-most powerful man in the country, known for his rough and ready methods.

I went to meet him and tried to explain the gist of my report. He seemed determined not to give credence to my submission and I came out of his office feeling rather defeated. I had to tell my boss what had transpired, which in effect, amounted to a total rejection of my report by the Home Minister. The Director gamely smiled and consoled me, saying I had done my best.

Though he may have given me that impression, fortunately for me, the seasoned Charan Singh did not summarily dismiss my submission. The Janata government had my report vetted by a reputed and perfectly impartial lawyer Mr Khandalwala, who emphatically endorsed my version.

In passing, I may add, the L.N. Mishra murder case has the historic achievement of being the longest matter with a pending judicial decision and was decided by a Delhi court in 2014, about 40 years after the bomb explosion that killed the minister.

The CBI stand has been vindicated and the eight accused from the Anand Marg sect have been convicted. It feels good that, finally, my report has been accepted by the highest law of the land. It came rather late, but eventually affirmed that the CBI was right.

'*Don't aim at success. The more you aim at it and make it a target, the more you are going to miss it. For success, like happiness, cannot be pursued; it must ensue, and it only does so as the unintended side effect of one's personal dedication to a cause greater than oneself or as the by-product of one's surrender to a person other than oneself. Happiness must happen, and the same holds for success: you have to let it happen by not caring about it. I want you to listen to what your conscience commands you to do and go on to carry it out to the best of your knowledge. Then you will live to see that in the long run—in the long run, I say!—success will follow you precisely because you had forgotten to think about it...'*

—Viktor Frankl, Austrian psychiatrist and survivor of Auschwitz

# 10

# Living in the Moment

*'In every outthrust headland,*
*in every curving beach,*
*in every grain of sand,*
*there is a story of the earth.'*

—Rachel Carson

**Prologue**

Since Barmer, the border town I was posted in as the SP, was facing a war situation for the first time during the 1965 conflict with Pakistan, the people in the district were understandably jittery, and what further aggravated the prevalent anxiety was the hyperactive media, which published fanciful imaginary stories with gleeful gusto, making enemy 'paratrooper' landings an ever-present threat, though there were only stray late-night para-droppings on the outskirts of some cities of Punjab. And in those cases, the paratroopers proved to be 'sitting ducks', landing almost literally into the laps of the vigilant people. Even before they could fold up their parachutes, they were captured and bundled off into improvised prison camps.

The local media, keen to build its readership during these sensational times when their news reports were most in demand, stoked Barmer's phobia by suggesting that the next target could well be Barmer town itself. Mercifully, the predictions did not come true, and barring some false alarms, Barmer district remained untouched by this potential menace.

As the war came to our sector, the media had managed to rouse fear and excitement to such a high pitch that it seemed almost unfair to deprive the citizens of the thrill of encountering a paratrooper. What I mean to say is that Barmer had been primed for what was to come and it wasn't entirely their fault when they were taken in by the rumour of a paratrooper landing in the middle of the town one night. So much so that the government machinery had to move fast to respond to this 'belief' before the paranoia got out of hand.

Returning from a late-night patrol, as I was about to hit the sack, I got a call and heard the excited voice of T.V. Ramanan, the district collector of Barmer, on the phone, 'Where've you been, dear fellow? I've been receiving frantic calls from the public. They keep on insisting that paratroopers have landed in the town. The SHO and DSP have evidently failed to allay their fear and the public are clamouring for action from us.'

'I am on my way,' I responded. After giving a forlorn glance at my empty bed and noticing that my wife and children were peacefully snoring, I went to the collector's residence, picked up Ramanan and drove to the spot—the spacious chowk of the main market, right in the middle of the town.

Our arrival was met with hushed silence, as the spokesman of the gathering, the chairman of the municipality, hurriedly approached us. It was still dark as dawn had not yet broken. He pointed at a high boundary wall behind which muffled sounds of someone trying to move could be distinctly heard. Then he said just one word in an awed whisper, '*chhatadhari* (paratroopers).'

Ramanan and I looked at each other. It was quite clear to us that the uncoordinated commotion on the other side of the wall lacked the measured rustle of an expert intruder in warfare. Moreover, paratroopers did not make landings in the middle of a bustling town, inviting immediate detection and capture. However, as the crowd's current frame of mind seemed unreceptive to logic, and as nothing less than a 'capture of the enemy' would satisfy them, I, torch in hand, climbed the wall. After all, in war times, we not only had to fight the enemy but also the perceptions that could sap the morale of the public.

---

As I climbed, there was no let-up of the suspicious sounds from the other side. Once on top of the wall,

I cautiously switched on my torch, shielding the glare with my palm, to locate the source of the noise. What I saw was an amusing sight—an excellent example of how phantoms can be cooked up in the dark if the atmosphere is sufficiently stoked.

It was a dog, frantically struggling to get out of a ditch half-filled with dried-up leaves. In the process, he was creating quite a racket. He must have fallen into it in the dark. On closer scrutiny, though, my hunch was proved wrong. It wasn't that he had been blinded by the darkness of the night. Something more weird had occurred. The dog's head was stuck in a narrow-necked earthen pitcher. It must have happened as he put his nose in, thinking there was food in the pitcher. Curiosity can kill a cat but for a dog, hunger is a more potent enemy. The dog was in quite a frenzy by now as its yelps for help were rebounding at him in a booming echo, driving the beast into a state of utter dread and despair.

I didn't have dogs as pets then and was a bit awkward around them but my concern for the beast overpowered my discomfort. I quickly acted, picking up a small stone and smashing the earthen pitcher. Vision restored, the dog stumbled out of the ditch and slunk away to safety. Climbing down the wall, I joined the waiting crowd with a warm smile. They had also seen the dog escaping in the darkness and the noise had abated. The totally abashed chairman of the municipality who had caused the action triggering off my climb on the wall, looked very contrite and apologized for the inconvenience. The crowd also looked ashamed of their unthinking panic.

I smiled and offered the chairman a face-saving response. Making light of the incident, I said, 'Sorry, friends, even if there was a *chhatadhari*, I guess he fled without introducing himself.' All the people gathered there fidgeted awkwardly in embarrassment and the chastened chairman tendered apologies for wasting our 'valuable time!' We shrugged it off with a 'What are we here for?'

In retrospect, however, we thought that it was not a total waste of our time. First, it was an intensely shared experience that convinced the public that the administration was always available to assuage their fears and doubts, howsoever unfounded.

Secondly, the incident helped to make the local leaders and the local press realize that the least they could do was to avoid diverting the hard-pressed administration into fruitless pursuits and that, for optimal utilization of available energy and resources, the district administration needed their thoughtful and constructive cooperation rather than a frenzied reaction to unusual situations. This incident achieved for us what perhaps intense sermonizing would have failed to do.

Thirdly, the people in the town had showed immense reluctance to jump into the trenches when the enemy planes flew overhead. We as officials would plead with them to follow our instructions for their own safety, but they would often argue about the need to do so. After this incident, the process became much smoother as they knew they could trust our judgement and needed to cooperate with us.

⁂

As a matter of fact, just as we were winding up the dog and pitcher operation with cheery Jai Hinds to each other, the red alert, by way of the hooting of sirens, warned us of danger. This had happened for the third consecutive night, indicating that hostilities were heating up in our sector too. We entered the nearest trench and stayed there for about 30 minutes, till the 'all clear' signal sounded.

I looked at my watch and frowned. The early hours of the morning were already on us and by the time I reached home, it was 4 a.m. I was literally dog-tired, and just had enough energy left to take off my beret, belt and boots, before crashing out for a quick nap.

I was lost to the world for a while, but soon I stirred uneasily and sat up bolt upright at realizing that I was the sole occupant of the bedroom. I shouted for the orderly and enquired about my near and dear ones. He sheepishly told me that they were in the trench!

'What? They are there still? Didn't they hear the "all clear signal"?' Saying nothing, he merely pursed his lips and looked down. I rushed to the trench outside. The dawn was just breaking and as the rays of the rising sun gently glided over the scene before me, I stopped in my tracks and stood rooted to the spot, totally entranced.

The family, *my* family, lay snugly on a neatly spread bedroll slightly jutting out of the trench. My wife lay sideways and her protective arm, enveloping the children, stirred in rhythmic motion in sync with their heartbeats. Seeing them snoring softly in perfect harmony and completely at peace, I smiled to myself and went back inside. Resisting the allure of my beckoning bed, I began my morning ablutions.

As my wife joined me for our morning tea, I said a cheery, 'Hello! Had a restful sleep?' Mrs Shiela Shekhar responded with a churlish grunt and, ignoring my sleep-deprived look, asked in return, 'And you?' I felt like grunting too, but refrained and said, 'Great! Whatever there was of it.'

She raised her eyebrows and fluttered her eyelids in confusion. I realized that she was still too drowsy to be fully aware of her surroundings

I smiled and said, 'Never mind. Incidentally the trenches can be put to optimal use only when people using them remain below ground level.'

She wasn't amused and gently rubbing her sleepy eyes, said, 'We are sick and tired of running to the trench when the sirens start shrieking, then trudging back to the bedroom after the "all clear" signal, and repeating the drill all over again at regular intervals in the night. And so, rather than lying awake waiting for the siren to wail, I decided to make ourselves comfortable in the trench itself.'

She had a valid point. Five-year-old Sanjeev and four-year-old Bharat could, no doubt toddle, though sleepily, along with her to the trench but Arjun, a bouncy baby aged barely five months, was at that growing phase when mother and child are more or less non-detachable items, and lugging him around even in normal circumstances was quite a daunting chore.

'Tell me, do the Pakis suffer from insomnia? Why do their planes make it a habit of flying over our town at all sorts of unearthly hours?' To emphasize her plight, she languidly stretched her limbs, gingerly rotated her neck, and visibly winced. I clucked in empathy as I massaged her neck and shoulders gently. Somewhat soothed by my gesture, she began the ritual of drinking her morning tea, reaching out for her exclusive cup and saucer, removing the tea-cosy from the teapot, and pouring out the steaming concoction. She proceeded to sip the tea daintily, slowly and sensually delighting in each tiny mouthful.

Well, I suppose there is a bit of a cat in every woman, just as there is a bit of a mouse in every man.

# 11

# The Tunnel to God

## Prologue

The pressure and stress of work had kept the SHO awake till the early morning hours. He walked into his office rubbing his tired eyes and hoping for some respite. But before retiring for the night, he decided to wind up his duties by having a peek at the *roznamcha*, which is a daily record of the duties and activities of a police station.

What he saw were mostly normal entries of civil disputes being sorted out, but one caught his attention. Being a seasoned sleuth, his hound-like nose began twitching as he read an account from a beat constable. The report pertained to a sadhu (a 'godman') who had walked into a village under his jurisdiction and 'adopted' it six months ago. This happened all the time and was nothing to get perturbed about, but what the report said next certainly was. The sadhu intended to perform a *samadhi* (a state of heightened spiritual consciousness reached after meditation, after which the 'enlightened' person leaves the body) as a parting gift for his devotees. The SHO knew perfectly well that a samadhi, shorn of its spiritual trappings, in plain speak is committing suicide!

❧

The SHO immediately set off to make enquiries. The sadhu and his entourage had set up their accommodation on the outskirts of the village. Not very far from it was a vast open space, at one end of which a square mud structure, about 3 feet high, had been constructed for use as a rostrum.The SHO could see the villagers gathered around it, festooning it with decorations. At the other end, just behind the rostrum about 15 feet away, was a small pit that had been dug and earmarked for the sadhu's samadhi. It was the trench in which he would be buried alive!

In an attempt to prevent the intended samadhi, the SHO tried to reason with Hetram, the sarpanch, telling him that what the sadhu intended to do was against the law and that his role as an abettor would make him equally liable to punishment. Hetram nodded in agreement but shrugged helplessly, using the time-worn ploy of consensus, 'Sir! I cannot go against the wishes of the villagers,' he said. The police officer told him that he was being evasive and irresponsible, but all he got in response was an even more pronounced shrug. The SHO was well aware of the hypnotic hold the purveyors of spiritual power had on the Indian public, more so on the people who lived in villages. Coupled with this truism was another indisputable fact, that the attempt to enforce law in the absence of social sanction was a tough proposition. Concluding that the situation was too hot to handle on his own, he contacted his Circle Officer, who, in turn, decided to inform me, the district SP.

I frowned. The samadhi could not be allowed to take place. However difficult it may be to enforce, I was determined that the law of the land must prevail. I, accordingly, worked out a strategy in consultation with my officers and contacted my boss, the DIG, to, inform him of the situation and to requisition more men to add to the already existing police force available in the district. The DIG agreed to send me more constables, but advised me to think about the option of non-intervention at this point and to resort to legal action only after the inevitable samadhi had occurred and the fervour of the people had died down.

'But Sir, I can't twiddle my thumbs while the law is being broken brazenly.' I wasn't much of a political animal and didn't see the need for his nuanced approach. 'It may hurt the reputation of the police if we let such an illegal action take place and later, it will go against us.'

'Well anyway, you are the man on the spot,' the DIG concluded, 'Try and avoid confrontation, if you can.'

The seasoned DIG had succeeded in making me realize that I had a choice. The obvious hitch was that allowing the event to take place would be seen as not only permitting the commission of a crime, just because we were under pressure, but also would demoralize anyone who thought the samadhi plan was unlawful and yet we let it happen.

Nonetheless, the talk with the DIG made me try a more subtle approach. I made an attempt to persuade the sarpanch, to make him realize that his own role as that of an abettor was wrong, but he said the villagers' had elected him and he could not go against the wishes of the majority.

I decided to go ahead with my original plan.

---

That night, sleep evaded me like an elusive criminal as I fretted over the prospect of my plan going wrong and the situation getting out of hand and exploding into a law and order problem of serious magnitude. And just as I was visualizing the consequences, I was startled by the incessant whirring sound of the intercom buzzer. Mrs Shekhar, my wife, although sufficiently accustomed to my late-night summons, stirred uneasily and mumbled, 'No, no, not yet. Wait for the third whistle before turning off the gas.' Then, apparently satisfied with her instructions, to 'whomsoever it may concern', she turned over to the other side to resume her beauty sleep. I smiled at the diversion and thanked God for small mercies. I picked up the phone. It was the DSP, saying he had some vital information and a visitor he wanted me to meet in the residential office.

What I found out that night changed my entire plan of action for the next day.

---

Cut to the day the sadhu is to go into his trance. The villagers have arisen early to congregate and hear his discourse just before he goes underground. As they eagerly await his arrival, they are talking in hushed whispers. It's a big spectacle, the first such for the village. The talk is centred around how the fortunes of the village will turn around due to the sadhu's choice of their humble abode for his great ascent to heaven. Someone puts on a loudspeaker that begins to spew out bhajans (devotional songs). The more devout begin swaying to the music.

Some of the villagers have lined up on the path leading from the hut that the sadhu has been living in on the outskirts of the village. Eventually, at dusk, he emerges from the hut and walks with long strides along the half a kilometre or so to the samadhi point. The villagers line up behind him and when they reach us, it's quite a sizeable group walking with a speed that means business.

As the sadhu reaches the spot, he waves cheerily to the crowd gathered there (every man, woman and child of the village is present) and folds his hands in the gesture of a *namaste* in response to their greetings.

He settles down, closes his eyes, gives a huge smile and after chanting some perfectly intoned shlokas, begins his sermon on, 'Truth is the ultimate winner'. Though his voice is high-pitched and shrill, he goes on to give a commanding oratorical performance that totally enthrals the audience.

Meanwhile, I reach the police outpost along with the CO, the SHO and the additional force. According to the plan, members of the detachment quietly position themselves at a distance behind the congregation. The sadhu notices the stirrings. He frowns and pauses. In unison, the crowd crane their necks as they turn to look back, unease writ large on their faces. Seeing this, the sarpanch climbs the platform and confidently assures the crowd. 'It is not unusual for the police to be present on such occasions. Please do not worry on that count.' He politely requests the sadhu to resume his discourse. The sadhu's stern face melts back into a benign smile.

His farewell talk is followed by laudatory speeches led by the sarpanch. The villagers take turns to lay their offerings at the sadhu's feet and receive his blessings. As the sadhu eats a frugal meal, the crowd watches in respectful silence.

As he slowly rises and begins his walk towards the trench, people push and shove each other to escort him and heap his frail body with garlands. He acknowledges their gestures with folded hands. Then he stops at the trench and turns to wave at the crowd, followed by a series of *namastes*. There is silence all around and saying that it is time for the sadhu to bid goodbye, his accomplices help him to step into the trench. Once the sadhu is sitting in the pit, they 'bury him alive' by piling spadefuls of mud over him. The spectators stand reverently with bowed heads but I notice that a small section of the crowd looks somewhat bemused at the police inaction, while others seem to have concluded that the police have chickened out.

As the last scoop of mud covers the sadhu, Vijai Kumar, the chief organizer of the sadhu's affairs, climbs the platform, looks defiantly at the police and thanks the crowd for their generous gifts. Then in solemn tones, he says: 'Dear friends, three days from now, on *Purnima* (full moon) day, we shall meet again to witness the ultimate *chamatkar* (miracle), when Mahatmaji will rise from his samadhi to bless you with his *darshan* (presence). Jai Guruji Maharaj!'

The crowd reciprocates with a resounding, 'Jai Guruji Maharaj'. The sarpanch embraces Vijai Kumar and both announce that they will be mounting a round-the-clock vigil around the samadhi area. I presume they are suspicious that the police will dig their ticket to publicity out of the hole.

The villagers return to their homes, looking ecstatic with their feeling of fulfilment, and the sarpanch is cock-a-hoop as he jauntily walks back along with his deputy sarpanch to their adjacent houses, where, not unexpectedly, a summons from the SP, me, awaits them. The sarpanch squirms as I take him to task. 'Hetramji, you think you are very clever. This fervour and frenzy will end in a few days and I am determined to wipe that smirk off your face. You just wait and watch!' The sarpanch's smile dissolves and he shakes his head in silence, managing to hide his elation at the SP's frustrated outburst. In his heart, he is, no doubt, thinking he has outwitted such a senior police officer and his achievement is going to launch his political career at the state level. At the very least, the ruling party would hear of his exploits.

Night has fallen. Three hours have elapsed since the start of the sadhu's underground sojourn. The village sleeps under the typical rural calm, occasionally broken by the shrill barks of the village dogs and the distant droning sounds of an approaching motor vehicle! A vehicle? Who could it be? I jerk myself out of a doze and tensely await the visitors. Could it be a higher ranking politician? Or a media hound from the town? We've tried to keep the story under wraps but the local media can sniff out a bone, however deep it's buried under the ground. The sarpanch and his deputy, who are keeping the vigil at the site along with us, also look surprised. Vijai Kumar and the other aides have gone back to the hut to get some sleep and they will take their place at the samadhi when dawn appears, as arranged by Hetram.

Thankfully, the vehicle turns out to be the CO's jeep. The officer alights and talks to me in whispers. I nod and walking up the sarpanch and his deputy, I ask them to climb at the back of the CO's jeep. After some hesitation, they get in and we head in the direction of the hut at the edge of the village from which the sadhu had emerged not long ago. It's about half a kilometre away.

When the sarpanch asks me where he is being taken, I tell him to wait and watch. The silhouette of the hut can be seen in the moonlit night, and its interior is hazily visible in the glow of the lantern. We get down at a safe distance and walk towards it. Organically, without my telling them, everyone is walking with silent stealth towards the hut. On reaching it, the police party gathers speed and makes a sudden entrance. Confused, the sarpanch and his deputy follow us quite swiftly, worried they may miss out on some action.

The inmates of the hut are a busy lot. One of the members of the sadhu's entourage is busy counting the cash offerings of the villagers, whereas the other one is tying up the gifts in a bundle. And, yes, the Sadhu Maharaj himself, with mud sticking to his body, is smugly reclining on a jute mat, happily puffing away at his 'chillum.'

One of his followers delicately kneads his calves. A bearskin hangs as a backdrop on the wall behind the sadhu. The inmates of the hut, with one exception, are all taken completely by surprise at our sudden entry. The exception is Vijai Kumar, the modern Judas, who stands reclining against the wall, with no expression on his face.

This sudden turn of events wipes the smug grin off the sadhu's face, which turns ashen. However, after the initial shock, he makes an amazing recovery, springs to his feet, turns around, pulls aside the bearskin and plunges headlong into the hollow cave freshly carved out in the wall—rather an impossible escape route to choose in the circumstances. The CO, hugely amused, bursts into a guffaw and says, 'Arre! Santji Maharaj! Wait! Wait! Don't be in such a hurry. I'm coming with you!' In one swift movement, he effortlessly grips the calves of the vanishing dervish and pulls him back into the hut.

The man still has fire in him. In an angry outburst, he says, 'You infidels! How dare you manhandle a saint? You all shall burn in the fires of hell.' His threat however, lacks conviction.

He was convicted in court for fraud not long after. And not just for the case in Hetram's village. It turned out he had duped a few other villages in the region too. The penitent sarpanch and his colleagues, who got their money and reputation saved by the skin of their teeth, attended every court hearing and rejoiced at the result. The star witness was the approver, Vijai Kumar.

What led Vijai Kumar to turn 'approver', and, in a manner of speaking, 'kill the goose that laid the golden egg?' Vijai Kumar was a jobless graduate with a sharp intellect but slothful ways. His father detested the idea of an educated but unemployed son whiling away his time at home, and made life miserable for him. So Vijai Kumar devised a diabolical scheme in which he had to have a collaborator.

In Hanuman Das, a *kathavachak* (scripture narrator), he found just the right man. Hanuman Das had only a working knowledge of the scriptures but was a gifted performer. All he needed was proper 'marketing' as a saintly sadhu and Vijai Kumar filled the void.

Their modus operandi was to meticulously reconnoitre villages (outside his home state of Uttar Pradesh in case he was recognized), consisting of a population of primarily gullible souls who had blind faith in practitioners of spirituality. His home state served the purpose of providing a shelter during the 'cooling off' period between what the gang called 'operations'.

Vijai Kumar would carefully gauge the village sarpanch's (headman's) reaction and, if he found him receptive, he would fix a date and schedule and then request him to provide accommodation to his group at the outskirts of the village. He would ask for a separate hut for 'Guruji', so that he could do his puja in serene, undisturbed surroundings. The arrival of the party would be followed by an announcement of the plan for the sadhu to take samadhi. And with his very first discourse, Hanuman Das would begin casting such a spell that by the end of it, throngs would literally sing to his tune.

Meanwhile, the followers would proceed to dig a trench or pit for all to see. And then, in the dead of night, they would extend the trench into a tunnel leading to the hut. Following the 'holy burial', Vijai Kumar, after allowing for a discreet time lapse, would give an agreed-upon sound signal and then, while the village slept, the sadhu would creep through the duct to enter the hut. The reunion would culminate in a short convivial rejoicing, followed by a clean getaway. And some very scary close calls notwithstanding, he and his group had hitherto managed to elude the police and remain one step ahead.

Coming back to the question of why Vijai Kumar busted his own racket and why he turned approver, this is what happened. Initially, the sharing of the bounty showered on them by unsuspecting villagers was on an equal footing between Hanuman Das and Vijai Kumar, both cornering the major share and leaving pitifully small amounts for the remaining three members who were a bunch of unskilled, unlettered and non-protesting 'tunnel diggers'. After a few exceedingly profitable outings, Hanuman Das, bitten by the bug, began disputing the rationale of the distribution, claiming that his share should be much greater. He argued that he was the one who took most of the risks and it was his oratory that won them the villagers' trust, and the size of their offerings was related to this trust. Though he knew that but for Vijai Kumar, he would have continued to barely scrape a living as a storyteller in a pandit's (temple priest's) entourage and that their daring and profitable escapades were largely due to Vijai Kumar's strategic planning, he bargained for more, saying he was the lion that the people saw and became in awe of and thus he must get the lion's share.

The animosity about the division of spoils grew between them and finally, when he couldn't bring his protégé round, Vijai Kumar was enraged. Hanuman Das, the creature of his inventive genius, had begun to have delusions about his own indispensability. The dispute about the distribution of spoils apart, Vijai Kumar had already begun doubting his faith in their invulnerability. Was all the risk worth it? The earlier close calls had badly shaken his belief. These were the reasons why he was so keen to extricate himself from this mess of his own making.

His state of indecision was finally resolved by an unexpected development. When the SHO returned from his first recce of the village, he had met Vijai Kumar. Soon after, Vijai Kumar came to the police station to pay him a courtesy call, and to gauge the SHO's attitude. He wanted to see if there was any danger of their plans being discovered and foiled.

The SHO, by then fortified by my backing as the SP, told him firmly that in no circumstances would an illegal act, such as a samadhi, would be permitted, and gave him such a menacing glare with a threatening stance that Vijai Kumar squirmed. This was the first time that any police officer had been that blunt and unambiguous.

And then, half-jokingly, the SHO remarked, '*Sadhu Maharaj ko samadhi ke jariye Bhagwan ke paas pahunchane ke liye surang mil gayee hai kya?*' (Has Sadhu Maharaj, through the means of his samadhi, found a tunnel to reach God?)

The unwitting mention of the word *surang* (tunnel) by the SHO opened the floodgates of admission. Guilt-ridden, full of resentment—and strangely relieved—Vijai Kumar decided to come clean then and there. The changed police strategy to nab the sadhu was based on Vijai Kumar's confession to the SHO, and, eventually, to me, the SP, at my residence.

Hanuman Das was sentenced to 18 years in prison while Vijai Kumar had a much shorter time to serve as a deal since he had turned approver. This time there was no tunnel out of the hole they had dug themselves in.

# 12

# Humour in Uniform

*Humour is another of the soul's weapons in the fight for self-preservation. It is well known that humour, more than anything else in the human make-up, can afford an aloofness and an ability to rise above any situation, even if only for a few seconds.* – Victor Frankl

On one occasion, when there was a virulent agitation by students in Jodhpur and they were on a rampage, the SP's presence on the scene became imperative. I rushed to the spot and found that the group of about 100 youngsters were in a very belligerent mood and, on my arrival, they began pelting missiles at me. They were students of Law College at Jodhpur and were agitating for upgrading the status of their college to a full-fledged university, an issue that could hardly be resolved in the streets but there it was—youthful energy and anger had to be released somehow and at that moment I, as the government's representative on the spot, became their lightning rod.

When an SP comes under fire, the constabulary's conditioned response is to raise their firearms and take aim at the offenders. And once policemen raise their rifles, even the protesters know that they have crossed a line and dire consequences are to follow. It was looking bad; tempers were flaring up all around but I didn't want young blood on my hands. According to me, it still wasn't a law and order situation that needed police firing. I asked my force to stand down and told them we would act with restraint. Though I was tense, I raised my arms in a gesture of placation, showing I was holding no weapons. I smiled at the students, and to draw their leader's attention, said, '*Judge Mahodaya, yeh mamlaa bina kisi jhagde ke sulajh sakta hai* (Mr Judge, this matter can be resolved without any quarrel). I assure you that, if need be, I shall intercede on your behalf before the authorities concerned.'

The keywords, in my invitation for negotiations were, of course, 'Judge Mahodaya.' I chose to address leader of the group in this way deliberately. He was a bearded but bewildered-looking young man who seemed to be uncomfortable with some of his more belligerent group members throwing stones at me. Realizing that their action had resulted in the policemen raising their guns against the protesters, he was trying to calm them down, just as I had done to my force, except that my men were used to following orders. He was remonstrating with some of the hotheads when he heard what I was saying to him.

Since they were law students, I was playing on the basic sense of law and order that they would have to maintain in their future roles. I wanted to remind them that they must not be disruptors and never take law in their own hands, however just they felt their cause was. All this I hoped would sink in by my calling their leader 'Judge Mahodaya'. And moreover, one mustn't forget that for a budding lawyer, the position of a judge is very aspirational. Of course, I saw all this rationalizing in the 20-20 vision of hindsight. At that moment, I'd just taken an instinctive risk. Luckily, it worked.

The student leader grabbed at the 'escape clause' I provided in the unwritten contract I was offering to him. He smiled back and announced to his group that he believed the matter was in good hands now and they should not agitate further. The crowd dispersed on this assurance and he and a few of his peers came to sit with me and talk about their grievances.

A very tense situation had been defused by my smile and light banter. As a matter of fact, my remark wasn't very far off the mark because that youth leader, Maghraj Kalla, did eventually went on to become a judge of the Rajasthan High Court; and, more significantly, our mutual regard for each other served us well throughout our careers. Neither of us had any hesitation in consulting each other as and when a situation arose. On one such occasion, he reminded me of this incident and told me how it had inspired him to use humour in his courtroom, especially when the arguments became heated. He told me how it worked like magic to defuse tense situations many times. Hearing him say this, of course, gave me great satisfaction.

# 13

# Encounter in London

## Caught by the Other Bobby

In 1973, I attended a short course on government administration in London. At the same time, a close friend, Rakesh Dayal, RD for short (name changed), my erstwhile batch and cadre mate in the IPS, was doing a long course at Oxford University, presumably a privilege he earned for ditching the IPS and joining the Indian Administrative Service (IAS). Evidently, IAS officers require a longer time to learn!

He had acquired a second-hand car, a Volkswagen, which surely must have seen better days in the distant past. But by the time the vehicle came into my friend's possession, it was already beyond redemption; it made such a racket that it was heard much before it was seen. Oxford, evidently, could afford to live with this nuisance.

One Sunday, he came to London to pick me up for a jaunt in his decrepit old jalopy. Seeing the battered condition of the car, I had second thoughts, but eventually I reluctantly agreed to go for the joy-ride for old times' sake.

I asked him, 'How come no Bobby has got after you?'

'How I wish she had...so cute she is.' At first I was puzzled, then I realized he was talking about Dimple Kapadia, who had starred in the film *Bobby* that had been released in Bollywood earlier that year and had made the actress the talk of town.

'The other Bobby, RD. You know who I mean, a London policeman. This jalopy of yours is a rattle bag. It looks so ramshackle and must be noisy, too!'

Genuinely hurt, he looked at me and said, 'What noise? My car runs smoothly, it just looks noisy. C'mon in. You'll see.'

My friend chose the busiest and most posh area of London, Piccadily, to start our sightseeing tour. Wrong choice. Because as I'd reckoned, Oxford being an academic's town, the police there may have tolerated his eccentric jalopy but it didn't go down well with the swarming Bobbies in Piccadily Square.

At once a cop stopped the car to haul my friend up. Frowning at him, he licked his pencil, all ready to give him a ticket for a hefty sum, which was equivalent to a week of our meagre daily allowances. I was horrified at the loss we would suffer and my mind somehow raced over all the loved ones back home I would miss getting gifts for. Somehow RD used all his convincing charm and managed to sweet-talk the Bobby into giving us an oral reprimand.

No sooner had we got away than RD's incessant chatter was cut short by the jalopy's horn. It started blaring without any provocation or touch and refused to stop, reminding me of my daughter Shalini as a toddler. This surprised RD even more than me because apparently he hadn't expected the fat lady to suddenly burst into song. The trip was far from over.

We could, no doubt, have parked the car, opened the bonnet and gagged the offending piece. But finding parking space in the busiest part of London was no easy task. And RD hadn't the foggiest idea about parking in London. So he circled the roundabout under the statuesque, though rather censorious glare of the 'Angel of Christian Charity', a sheepish look on his face.

His predicament was temporarily resolved by two police cars piloting and escorting him to a side street. A policeman dashed to the bonnet and fiddled with the mechanism there, managing to silence the horn. Then, when the traffic in charge brought out his ubiquitous notebook, for once my friend had nothing to say. His horn had done the talking already.

The traffic cop, with an amused look, asked my friend for the car papers and proceeded to clamp a stiff fine. Then with a broad grin, he said, 'Sorry to have interrupted your sightseeing, Sir! Please feel free to resume your Piccadily Circus circuit along with your friend—but on foot, if you please. Your repaired car will be sent to your address at Oxford.'

Generally unflappable, RD, for once, looked rattled. There was nothing he could do but grin and bear it. Shifting uneasily from one foot to another, he said a 'sorry' to me, not to the Bobby.

I gently patted him on the back and said, 'Come over to my room, and let's have a cup of hot tea.' I had been allotted a room in one of the hotels abutting Kensington Gardens in Hyde Park.

After a sip or two, my pal was back in his element. He started with a tentative smile and then burst out in unrestrained laughter. 'Ha! Ha! Ha! These Bobbies think they are very smart. Now they are going to foot the bill for the repair of my jalopy and for the fuel too.'

He was wrong by a mile. The London police had 'the last laugh'; they did get the jalopy repaired but sent the bill to my friend Rakesh Dayal, who had to pay an amount that far surpassed the price he had paid to buy the dilapidated car!

# 14

# Catching Up with Greed

*'Vultures so drunk on flesh that they sat lopsidedly on roof-tops, waiting for appetite to return.'*—Salman Rushdie in his book, *Moor's Last Sigh*

I was posted on deputation as the SP of the CBI, Jaipur Branch, in June 1972 after a continuous stint in the state police for about 14 years. I was quite aware that it required back-breaking effort and was prepared for it. I worked hard to learn the ropes about functioning on the 'chair' where I was destined to spend long hours.

Among the first things I did was to catch up on matters pending decision. So I called DSP Mahendra Singh and asked him to brief me. The list was long but the most important matter was regarding the chief engineer of the Khetri Copper Project, who had demanded a bribe for certifying the completion of work of a private contractor. The importance of the matter was mainly due to two aspects: the amount demanded (Rs 5,000) and the rank of the person (chief engineer) asking for the bribe. In 1972, this amount was substantial, unlike today when even a traffic cop would pocket it for a small road transgression. The bribe hadn't yet been taken but the complainant claimed that he had been asked to give it soon. It is a crime to demand a bribe but unless money actually exchanges hands, it may be difficult to prove.

I was not puzzled about why this case had been pending for a long period prior to my joining the branch. I felt that if there was hesitation on my predecessor's part, it was perhaps due to the matter being red-hot (a very senior government official was involved, after all) and because the case could not be prosecuted successfully without the actual exchange of money. I gave strict instructions to Mahendra Singh to locate the complainant without further delay and to ensure that he met me in the office.

DSP Mahendra Singh did the needful. When I met the complainant, a short fellow dressed all in white, even down to his shoes, with close-set eyes and dishevelled hair, I asked him: 'Was this the first time that you have been asked for a bribe?'

He replied, 'No. I've been asked to give a bribe before but I've never complied.' He looked up at the ceiling, reflecting for a moment, and then went on. 'But I thought, enough is enough. I've finished the work I was under contract for and was entitled to get a completion certificate and my payment. Why should I give a cut of that to the chief engineer? Someone has to bring the greedy to book. But it's been such a long delay and even the CBI has sat on my complaint.'

I told him the honest truth. 'You see, the person you want to bring to book is a high-ranking official, which in reality means that a mere verbal complaint won't work.'

He didn't bat an eyelid before responding, 'We can catch him red-handed then.' He sounded very determined, unwilling to let this matter rest. So we decided to take action, and then and there, the plot to catch the culprit actually accepting the bribe was born.

In those days, Delhi had two five-star hotels—Ashoka and Akbar—owned by the Indian Tourism Development Corporation (ITDC). According to the plan, the complainant contacted the chief engineer in question and said that he was ready to pay the bribe. The chief engineer asked the complainant to meet him at the Akbar Hotel and hand over the sum demanded. It seemed the suspect used this hotel as his temporary residence whenever he stayed in Delhi.

The complainant informed us that the suspect would take his bribe a week later after arriving in Delhi by the evening plane from Madras (the name for Chennai in those days). He had booked a room on the fifth floor.

When I informed DIG Jagadanand over the phone about the plan, I could sense a lack of enthusiasm in his response. I could understand his hesitation, thinking (probably rightly) that it was sheer bravado on the part of a rookie, an officer on deputation to one of the state branches of the CBI for the first time—who had no clue of how the CBI functioned at the national level—to suggest such an audacious plan.

He asked me crisply, 'Hasn't anyone advised you against it?'

I said, 'No, on the contrary, DSP Mahendra Singh thinks it's a good idea.'

'That's why I'm against extending that fellow's deputation to the CBI. He's an ass. Don't you both realize that the suspect is a very high-ranking national government official? If your "operation" doesn't succeed, the CBI will have a lot of egg on its face!'

When I met the DIG in Delhi, he was still sceptical and again hinted that the decoy plot we had hatched was very bold and ambitious. He said that usually the CBI worked behind the scene and our plan to lay a trap was more of a field officer's way of doing things. He added, 'Mahendra Singh should have advised you correctly.'

I held firmly to my stance, replying, 'It was my idea, not Mahendra Singh's. I decided on this course of action after I spoke with the complainant, who looked like he could play the part correctly and was, in fact, determined to expose the corrupt man.'

When he saw how keen I was, the DIG reluctantly gave the green signal but with the clarification that it was only on my insistence, making it seem that he was washing his hands off the operation. His qualified nod made me nervous for the first time, and I discussed the matter with my team consisting of the seasoned DSP Mahendra Singh and two inspectors, one of whom was a direct recruit of the CBI and had a workable knowledge about important locations in Delhi, Akbar Hotel being one of them. I was no stranger to Delhi either since I had studied in a residential college in Delhi. Moreover, I had taken the precaution of arriving three days before the date and had done some recce with my team. My family had come along with me as my wife's family lived there. They had been surprised when I offered to take them with me, and the response to my declaration that we were going to Delhi the next week were quizzical looks because it would normally take several rounds of requests for me to agree to take out time from my work schedule in Jaipur to make a trip to Delhi. Of course, as was the protocol for a secret mission, they had no clue why I had the sudden urge to visit Delhi.

Since the site of the trap was the government-owned Akbar Hotel, we as government authorities had no difficulty in getting the cooperation required from the manager. He not only showed us the room booked by the suspect but, on our request, provided us with two hotel employees to act as eyewitnesses.

The complainant met us in the hotel and we went to the fifth floor room with him. Although the room was quite spacious, the lobby outside it was not, and this factor was a big handicap since the plan was to place our team, along with the two witnesses, in the lobby. Since it was so small, it would entail six of us jostling shoulders in a terribly constricted space.

Nonetheless, the advantage was that the curtain of the anteroom abutting the suspect's was translucent, thus allowing a clear view of the interior of the room from an angle in the lobby whereas the occupant would have to draw the curtain on the main window in his room to look out at that area. We tried to make the arrangement foolproof by instructing the complainant not to tinker with the drawn curtain on the room window nor let the suspect inadvertently do so.

On the decided date, in accordance with the plan, the complainant met the suspect in the hotel reception and accompanied him in the elevator to the room on the fifth floor. Apparently, the suspect was in a good mood, according to the complainant when we met him later, humming to the tune of the song he began playing on his tape recorder. He was a tall fellow who stooped and walked with a slight limp. When he walked to the window to draw the curtain, the doughty complainant knew he had to act swiftly, or we would be discovered hiding in the ante room. With remarkable alacrity, he whipped out a neatly bound pack of notes from his pocket.

To his relief, the suspect turned around from the window and greedily seized the packet, shoving it into an inner pocket of the loose coat he was wearing. He said, 'You are in a hurry to get to the point, aren't you?' Then in a rare gesture for a bribe-taker, he bowed politely and said, 'Thanks. Would you care to have a cup of tea? You can then tell me what took you so long to agree to my small request.' He smiled at the complainant.

He was about to order tea when the complainant gave the signal, a knock on the window, for us to enter. We rushed in, challenged the suspect and asked him to hand over the bribe money. Caught red-handed, he had no choice but to comply.

DIG Jagadanand was mighty pleased that we had managed to spring the decoy trap without anything going wrong. He congratulated me profusely. After a pause, he told me, 'The Director of the CBI is waiting for you.' This was big! News of my proactive measure must have reached the Director, a kind of operation which the CBI usually didn't get their hands dirty on.

DIG Jagdanand continued, 'Please remember, Mr Sen is a man of few words. He is totally focused on work and has no time for niceties. He expects similar conduct from visitors.'

I thanked the DIG and stepped out of his room for my first face-to-face interaction with the formidable Devendra Nath Sen.

As I entered, Mr Sen looked at me, nodded and silently pointed to the chair facing him. When I sat down, he said, 'Good work.' With due modesty, I said, 'Thank you, Sir.' In the absence of any further reaction from him, I began wondering whether this was the end of the session and should I get up and politely exit. However, before I could do that, he said in a balanced tone, 'Your record in the state is satisfactory, but it would be wrong of you to think that you will automatically do well in the CBI. There is a lot of difference between the working style of organizations and the key to success lies in your being able to adapt to the work culture of the organization you have opted for. I am presuming that you already know what the difference is.'

I nodded silently.

Finally, he said, 'All right then. Anything else?'

I hesitated a bit and then told him that our DSP Mahendra Singh, on deputation from the state, had done commendable work in the operation, and even otherwise was doing well in the branch. 'Sir, his period of deputation is ending soon, but he is keen on an extension. May I request you to let him continue for another six months?'

He glared at me. I suddenly felt that I had shot off my mouth and perhaps jeopardized, rather than helped, the cause. Mr Sen stayed silent for a while and then said, 'This Mahendra Singh seems very eager to do a good job.' Having said that, he turned towards some files on his desk. Our interaction had clearly ended. I got up, came to attention and said, 'Thank you, Sir.' Then I went straight to the DIG's room.

He seemed to be anxiously awaiting my return and when I told him in detail about my interaction with Mr Sen, the DIG raised his eyebrow and said, 'I appreciate your guts for making the request to give Mahendra Singh an extension! But, if anything, he is sure to get marching orders at once. Amazing that the Director actually said you'd done "Good work". He never compliments an officer unless he has served for several years in the CBI.' Finally, ungrudgingly, he added, 'Congratulations, you are destined for a long innings in the CBI—though I am not sure of Mahendra Singh.'

Back in Jaipur, my orderly called me into the home office for a call late in the evening. 'DSP Sahib wants to talk to you. Said it's urgent.' In my mind, I thought 'That's the end of Mahendra Singh!' I'd grown to like him and depend on him and would be sorry to see him go. Despondently, I picked up the receiver and said,

'Hello,' in a heavy voice. But I was in for a surprise as it was an elated Mahendra Singh who told me that he had got the desired extension. 'Orders from the top, Sir. Thanks to you.' I realized that my bold action in carrying out the decoy trap had obviously earned the tacit endorsement of the Big Boss. He was a man of few words, but his unexpressed support was worth much more.

# 15

# Corruption Starts at Home

## Prologue

When I became the Director General of the Anti Corruption Bureau (DG ACB), Rajasthan, it was not my first posting in the ACB. My first transfer to the ACB came about in the most abrupt manner.

On a routine inspection, Hanuman Sharma, the then DG ACB visited Hanumangarh, Ganganagar, where I was posted as the assistant superintendent of police (ASP), Hanumangarh. He visited my office and said that Hanumangarh was a very important subdivision of the Ganganagar district, but known for violent crime and ridden with corruption, even among the police. He warned me that I should be proud of getting this posting but that I should tread the path of policing with caution.

Soon after, I received orders for my transfer from Hanumangarh to the ACB, Jaipur—all of a sudden, without any preamble. I suspected that Hanuman Sharma was behind the transfer and wondered whether it was because he found my work good or it was a punishment posting for something amiss under my jurisdiction in Hanumangarh.

❧

The first thing that I did after reporting on duty was to approach Hanuman Sharma and ask him what this sudden transfer implied. 'Were you unhappy with my work in Hanumangarh?'

'No. Not really,' he said in his casual, nonchalant manner, dismissing me with a wave of the hand.

'Why the abrupt transfer then?' I persisted. 'And why bring me to your department?'

'Okay, if you must know, there are two parts to it. The bad part is your penchant for *desi ghee* (homemade butter)!'

I was taken aback as I'd no clue what he was referring to.

He went on to explain. 'During my visit, I was told that you had asked an inspector who was proceeding on leave to his village famous for pure *desi ghee*, to bring some for you.'

'But I gave him advance payment for it,' I said indignantly.

'That's what saved you. And yet it was a personal request, a favour. Though not corrupt in itself, it can be deemed as a precursor of possible corruption!'

At first, my head swam on hearing his allegation. I'd not meant it like that at all! He paused to allow me to digest what he had said. And when I was able to understand his comment, I realized he was right.He continued, deducing from my expression that I'd got the point, 'And the best way for "course correction" was to remove you from there and take you under my wing because I see a lot of potential in you.'

When, much later in my career, I became the DG ACB, I kept Hanuman Sharma's squeaky clean image in my mind, his high ideals were reinforced in me by a framed photograph of Mahatma Gandhi on my office wall.

One day, I was busy discussing pending cases with some officers when my PA, personal assistant, informed me on the intercom that Buta Singh, the Union home minister, wanted to speak to me on the phone. It was an extraordinary situation as it was not the practice for a Central Home Minister to call a DG ACB directly—he is supposed to approach the chief minister of the state first as a matter of protocol.

Buta Singh turned out to be a softspoken person and began by asking me about my welfare. When I replied that all was well with God's grace, he grunted as a preamble to what he was going to say. 'I'm calling about a case of illegal gratification.' These may not have been his exact words but I recall he didn't use the words 'bribe' or 'corruption'.

He said that a case had been registered against Mahender Singh (name changed), the tehsildar of Jalore. I remember noting at that point that Jalore was Buta Singh's constituency. Things started to fall in place and the reason for the call became clear even before he stated it. 'The man is innocent and action may be taken to exonerate him.' After a pause to take in the blatant interference with the executive process, I said that I would look into the matter.

Immediately afterwards, I called in the DSP who was investigating the case and asked to see the relevant file. Even before we could start the discussion, all of a sudden there was a commotion. Barging into my office without a 'by your leave' was a person I'd never seen before and who had the temerity to push anyone who tried to stop him from coming into my office, unannounced. To my utter amazement, the stranger plonked himself on the chair opposite me.

In a belligerent voice, without much ado, he said, 'You must have received a call from Buta Singhji. I want to know if you have taken action in compliance with his order.'

Outraged at his aggressive behaviour, I said, '*Khada ho aur nikal ja bahar abhi* (Get up and leave my room at once)!' The man looked stunned but seeing the rage on my face, complied with alacrity.

It was none other than the tehsildar Buta Singh had talked to me about. Despite his barging in unceremoniously, I later looked into the case with the DSP. After processing it and examining it meticulously,

I found him culpable and fit for being chargesheeted. I passed the order there and then, before any other calls came and got the file off my desk as soon as I could.

I don't know how Buta Singh took my stance in dealing with the case. However, when I didn't get marching orders within the next six months, I breathed a sigh of relief. Maybe he had himself processed the case and found he was backing a corrupt man.

# 16

# Man with a Mission

Just as I was about to lock my briefcase to wind up for the day, my gaze went to a couple of life insurance policies that I was to take a decision on. Mr Arya, the persistent Life Insurance Corporation (LIC) agent, had left them with me earlier. I bought these policies from him mostly because I liked the fellow's commitment and not because I necessarily thought they were needed. Where these policies were concerned, I wasn't sure at all that I would go in for them because I already had premiums to pay and my meagre salary as a police officer could not be stretched any further on savings. And yet, I'd kept the policies when Mr Arya insisted that this particular scheme had never been offered by any insurance company in the world and that I would be a fool to not at least consider them. I smiled at the memory of his hard selling. I have no head for figures and had no intention of scrutinizing the policies and comparing them with the others, but I'd kept them in my briefcase all the same, if only to keep Mr Arya's spirits up. Later, I could always decline saying that though I saw their value, I really didn't have the extra income to buy these new policies.

While I was mulling over my response to Mr Arya, my intercom buzzer rang. It was a call from Ganesh Singh, Additional Inspector General of Police (AIG), who supervised matters pertaining to personnel in the state police force, and I, as the Assistant Inspector General (AIG II) force, was his direct subordinate.

'Could you please come over? I need to discuss something urgent,' he said in his customary cool manner. Urgent staff jobs were generally nothing more than the preparation of statistics pertaining to the staff's capacities, transport facilities, weaponry and allied paraphernalia. It entailed some pressure but no tension as such, except that it was irksome when the work clashed with my now closed briefcase.

At times, in a bout of pique, I would feel that my boss deliberately invented urgent jobs, or, for variety, gave ordinary jobs an air of urgency just to keep me tethered to my desk beyond regulation hours.

The request must be from the state cabinet, I guessed, and would be sufficiently vague, prompting us to give all kinds of data rather than something specific. The Chief Minister perhaps delighted in keeping his ministers guessing, so he generally refrained from spelling out the exact topic for discussion, saying he wanted a discussion on the police force early next day, mentioning words like 'deputation', 'crime situation', 'allowances,' and so on.

The home minister, whose position in the ministry was shaky at best, would take no chance and hence requisition a plethora of data, which required reams and reams of paper work, the bulk of it perhaps futile.

Be that as it may, I picked up my notebook and climbed the stairs to my boss's office. He was scowling at the wall facing him, and I imagined he, too, was as miffed at the last-minute request, for a change.

As I entered, he subjected me to a penetrating look, and sternly asked, 'When are you going to get your hair cut?'

I had worked in a number of districts on the trot—as a matter of fact at a gallop—and this was my first staff job at the police headquarters after about 11 years of inspecting police offices, police lines and police parades in a 'regulation' crew cut. And to celebrate the change from that routine, I had indulged myself a bit and let my hair grow.

'Tomorrow, Sir...,' I blurted out. His frown melted into a benign smile.

'Yes, looks like today we will keep you busy till late in the evening . The secretariat officials want the strength of the IPS cadre, posting of IPS officers on deputation and those among them who have overshot the period of deputation. And yes, also the names of officers who had applied to go on deputation. I believe you are one of them,' he smiled again. 'Finally, and most significantly, just give them anything else that has to do with deputations.'

Responding to my bemused look, he said, 'I know, I know. The home department should already be in possession of all the details but I suppose they don't want be caught on the wrong foot. And, yes, I also know that even in our office, this actually is the task of the AIG I. But, of course you know, he is on leave. For that matter, so is the IGP himself.'

He waved his hands and gave me a helpless look. I shrugged, went back to my desk and applied myself to the onerous task of pre-computer days, when ledgers and files would have to be opened and notes dictated to a stenographer. I called the missing AIG I's personal assistant and told him to trace some papers. It was going to be a long night, so I rang up home to prepare my actual home minister.

I could sense the beginning of a frown and some heavy breathing at the other end.

I laughed nervously. 'Ha! Ha! You sound like you know why I'm calling. Some last minute work. Ha! Ha!'

To which her response was, 'So what's new? Ha! Ha!'

Anyway, to work out the frustration while I waited for the AIG I's PA to find the relevant files, I stepped out into the quadrangle just outside my office and launched into a rigorous walk, an exercise schedule I tried to adhere to, come what may. As I completed my second lap, the office orderly handed me a paper slip. There was someone to see me. 'At this late hour, who could it be?' I thought to myself, at first viewing the intrusion with annoyance. Then I saw the name of the visitor and brightened up.

I saw the pleasant, familiar face of Mr Arya, the LIC agent, who had struck a good rapport with me during my posting in the Jalore district. As I said before, among his many sterling qualities was his indefatigable spirit, his perseverance and persistence—and I don't mean just in the matter of selling his policies. He was born with a stump instead of a left wrist due to which his successive applications for a driving licence had been refused by my predecessors, and rightly so. Yet he came to us again and again. On his nth attempt last year, when I became responsible for licences as one of my portfolios in Jalore, I had looked at him, rather, at his left arm, and politely declined with a smile.

He looked momentarily dejected but I knew he wasn't going to give up so easily. 'Sir, try me out. Give me a learner's licence and have me tested after the stipulated period before giving me the proper licence. I promise not to disappoint you.' He sounded so pathetic. 'You have seen me play tennis, no?'

That made me think. I *had* seen him play at the Jalore club and he was really agile. He would 'cup' the ball in his left stump, throw it up in a perfect trajectory and come up with a stunning first serve. More so, his volleys were almost unplayable.

I changed my mind at this recollection. 'Okay, let me give you the benefit of the doubt. No harm in letting you try with a learner's licence. But when you apply for the proper driver's licence, I will test you personally, all right?'

'You are great! No other officer has given me a chance.' He was ecstatic. 'Just you wait, Sir, I won't let you down. You won't regret this.'

And I didn't. He passed the final with merit and I had no qualms issuing him the licence that was his due. I remember him caressing it as if it was a rare gift and saying, 'The LIC gives an almost interest-free loan to buy a jeep. I can now apply for it. Thanks to you, Sir, and, of course, the Lord above.'

From then on, he was his own driver right until he, unfortunately, got laid up with renal failure. Driving his own vehicle added to his sales capacity hugely as he could travel faster and to far-flung regions. He became easily the best sales representative the LIC ever had in that region! I say this from the evidence of my personal experience since he'd managed to con me into insuring every member of my family, with the sole exception of our pet parakeet. This bird had, incidentally, taken an instant dislike to Mr Arya, I suspect because Arya could easily out-talk the garrulous bird.

---

That evening, in the gathering twilight, as I walked into my room, still awaiting the AIG I's PA who was to get me the required data, Mr Arya rose from the chair and greeted me with his trademark smile, like a car headlight in its full beam.

'How come you are in Jaipur?'

'To meet you, Sir.' I wondered how many people he had given that line. He added, 'I have something for you.' I became wary, thinking of the wares he would ply me with, as I had still to make up my mind about the policies in my briefcase. Mercifully though, Mr Arya was not on a mission to further secure my family's future. He was, at that moment, simply a harbinger of good news and acting as a messenger for one of his clients. As was his wont, he began talking even before he sat down. '*Bhai Sahib, aap kaise hain?* (Brother, how are you?) And Shiela Bhabhiji and your entire family? You are looking in good health, thanks be to the Lord above!'

I replied quickly, 'Fully insured, all of us, therefore tension-free, thanks be to you and, of course, the Lord above.'

He laughed obligingly and said, 'You remember Guptaji, the public works engineer?'

Noticing my blank expression, he said, 'Parmesh Chand Gupta, Sir! He played tennis with us! Of course, not regularly since he was busier measuring road widths; counting funds available and other such matters.' Nudged by a faint recollection, I nodded tentatively.

'Well Sir, after you left Jalore, he also went away. No, chucking up his job had nothing to do with your transfer, though like most of us, he also felt a void with you gone.' I coughed and mumbled my thanks. 'In fact, Guptaji discovered to his delight that he had saved enough money to shift to Bombay and become a film producer.'

I recalled that Gupta had enjoyed a background of wealth, but was known to have other dubious dealings to further augment a decent bank balance.

Arya apparently guessed my line of thought and said in a somewhat mysterious manner, 'Sir, you know the saying, "wealth begets wealth"... Anyway, I had gone to Bombay to follow up the premiums of policies I had sold to him and some others. Guptaji gave me the good news that his daughter was getting married. He remembered you fondly and gave me an invitation card for you—and that's why I'm here.'

At that moment, the AIG I's PA knocked and entered the room. I gave him the necessary instructions while Arya rummaged in his bag. He brought out an ornate envelope with a gold-laced border and handed it over to me. It was a bit too heavy for an ordinary wedding invitation. I opened it and was astonished at what I saw.

It was a metal slab that on close scrutiny happened to be a compact silver plaque of approximately 2 inches by 4 inches. A message was etched on it. Noticing my puzzled expression, he smiled and said, 'Read it, Bhai Sahib!'

The glittering invitation card blatantly flaunted Gupta's quantum jumps into the world of further affluence. I was rather repulsed by the vulgar display of wealth. I told Arya that it would not be possible for me to attend the auspicious occasion, but I would send a congratulatory letter. Arya nodded and was about to get up when he seemed to remember something, 'Bhai Sahib, you recall...' And from the mad gleam in his eyes, I knew that he was about to launch on a sales pitch. And I prepared myself for the unpleasant task, knowing full well that my present state of finances could certainly not afford an additional LIC policy.

Just then I heard the apologetic cough of the AIG I's PA and the whispered request for some clarification. I grasped at the opportunity and told Arya, 'We can discuss this some other time.'

Arya rose and said, 'Never mind, Sir. Even so, I'll leave the papers with you for perusal at your leisure.'

It was his 'never say die' streak coming to the fore. I didn't have the heart to remind him that another set was lying in my briefcase so he handed me a sheaf of papers and went away, a little crestfallen.

An insurance man always makes a comeback. He may not get business at a particular moment, but he leaves only after sowing the seed for future—and then returns to gauge whether the seed sown has sprouted. Mr Arya re-entered my room following a polite knock within five minutes of leaving.

He coughed, hummed and hawed, and I thought that even for an action-oriented man like Arya, it was rather presumptuous of him to think that I had already decided to accept his new proposal.

He said, 'Sir! I am sorry to have barged in, but I forgot to take your blessings.'

I laughed and said, 'I thought it was the young couple that needed them!'

'Of course, they too,' he said. 'The bridegroom is the son of a renowned financier and producer of films. I have already sounded Guptaji and he has promised to help me enter the profitable world of film insurance. I need your blessings for this new venture. There is quickly growing competition now to the LIC. I'm not able to sell as many policies now.'

I was stunned. He was a super salesman and had been awarded the 'Best Agent' trophy in the region twice in succession, had earned double increments, and was due for promotion. On the other hand, his success in the new venture was by no means assured.

Leaving behind a secure, rewarding job with the LIC, he was opting for 'the city of dreams', dreams that in most cases remained unfulfilled.

I couldn't help saying, 'About this new policy proposal, please tell me more about it. Is it the same one you left with me the last time?'

He stared at me for a while in surprise. I explained, 'You wanted my blessings? Then accept them. I'm buying one of these policies from you. Please make up the appropriate papers.'

His body relaxed and his face brightened as he said, 'I think I will stay on with the LIC. With God's grace, and that of customers like you, it will work out.' The full beamed smile lit me up from inside.

**Postscript:** It broke my heart when I learnt that within a month of his visit to Jaipur, Mr Arya died of renal failure and the new life policy that I took from him was the last one he sold.

# 17

# The Chief Chef

## Prologue

Since I am going to write on the relationship between the Collector of a district and the Superintendent of Police in this story, perhaps the serious-minded professional may get riled when I talk of its lighter side. But then, that is the charm of a district posting, the capacity to have an enduring partnership with a colleague even though it might involve compromises.

Though the mortal remains of the collector I speak of have been buried for a long time, he survives through two notable traits: his name and his culinary expertise. Whether it was a quirk of fate or a preposterous joke deliberately played on him by the ruling dispensation, it is a matter of recorded state chronicles that Rajasthan did have an IAS officer named Alauddin Khilji, whose last posting, before his retirement, was as the Collector of Chittorgarh (also Chittor or Chittaurgarh) district. But, of course, he neither had the untrammelled authority nor the inhuman ruthlessness of his namesake invader who had, as a matter of fact, ravaged the kingdom of Chittor, in what could be termed as one of the darkest phases of India's medieval history. You would have all heard of the time Rani Padmini, the queen of ruler Ratan Singh, burnt herself in the practice called *jauhar* in which women jumped into a pyre to protect their honour, rather than become a part of Khilji's harem after he had conquered Chittor.

The modern-day Khilji, the Collector of Chittor, fully appreciated the weight that history had put on him and he went out of his way to convince the public that history was not going to repeat itself. Let me put it on record that Alauddin Khilji, IAS, despite his name, had an unblemished career and retired as a successful bureaucrat with an unsullied reputation.

---

The story I want to tell is about his posting prior to Chittor where he and I crossed knives, in a manner of speaking. Before Chittor, he was the Collector of Jhunjhunu district. A seasoned campaigner nearing the end of his professional career, he was already in harness for some time before I, a raw officer who had completed only seven years of service (two of which had been spent in training), joined the district as the SP. Our first encounter itself set the pattern for subsequent ones.

The SP's office was in a separate wing in the Collectorate complex. After taking over charge, as I sat deliberating on when to pay the customary courtesy call on the Collector, a short-statured, dark-complexioned and exceptionally rotund man barged into my office unannounced, his paunch preceding him by about a yard! With ungainly pouches under his eyes, his chubby face was pockmarked. All in all, he created a rather poor first impression. But when his face lit up with a smile, it displayed the most remarkable feature of his personality—his strikingly expressive eyes. It was as if, in a stage play, a bright backdrop had suddenly outshone a black and white frontispiece.

'Welcome to Jhunjhunu, SP Sahib,' he said with an expansive spread of his arms. 'I thought I would spare you the formality of calling on the Collector first. I am Alauddin Khilji, Collector and District Magistrate of Jhunjhunu. Funny name isn't it? Jhunjhunu?' Khilji Sahib was perhaps acutely aware of the curiosity his name would evoke and thus had patented this deflecting ploy. I say this because I heard him use it elsewhere later.

His unprecedented initiative in calling on me first and his chameleon-like transformation from a nondescript person to a fascinating one caught me unawares, and after some confused hesitation, I rose and warmly shook hands with him.

He slouched comfortably into the seat offered by me and mumbled something that got lost between his

Adam's apple and double chin. As I begged his pardon for not visiting him first, I noticed that my formal tone made him sit up and gawk as if he had encountered an unfamiliar animal in a zoo. Recovering fast he said, 'I believe your family will join you later. If so, why don't you come over to my place for your evening meal?'

This offer rubbished all the lessons of etiquette that we had sedulously imbibed during our formative years of training at the Central Police Training College (CPTC) in Mount Abu, Rajasthan. We had been firmly told by our deputy commandant, Mr Stracey, that in official relationships, lest it be thought presumptuous, an invitation to share a meal should be made only after a decent gap followed a formal introduction.

But, of course, formality had already been dispensed with by Khilji Sahib when he entered my office unannounced. Moreover, since I had spent about five years in the state of Rajasthan with its ambience of decorum, so I was amazed at the unconventional strain shown in the Collector's behaviour, ignoring the bureaucratic unwritten rules, which forced me to drastically revise the theories of etiquette taught in my initial training period. I realized that many senior officers also paid little heed to these 'rules'.

A striking instance exemplifying this casual camaraderie was at the State Police Wrestling Meet when I had just completed two years of service in the state. I was totally flummoxed by the suggestion that the tournament be inaugurated with a bout between the 'top boss', the IG of the state, and I, the ASP, a mere probationer. The suggestion was mooted by none other than the 'top boss', the 'Chief' himself.

There was an awkward silence followed by a wave of nervous giggles all round as I mulled over the shocking anti-norm poser. The fact that he was imposingly well-fed vis-à-vis my lean and hungry frame, provided me with an escape route. I said, 'Sir! There would be a problem since the rules do not permit "featherweights" to be pitted against someone in the"super-heavyweight category".' The IGP burst into a hearty guffaw and heaving a sigh of relief, I remember not only joining in the mirth but laughing the loudest.

So, when Khilji made the offer, instead of trying to be circumspect in accordance with Stracey's training, I gratefully accepted his invitation.

'Good, good!' he exulted and giving me an intense look, he asked, 'So what is your choice, red or white?' he asked.

Funny chap, I thought, asking me my colour preference just like that! Anyway, I decided to play along and said, 'Green.' His puckered lips twisted into a grin and he said, 'No, no. I meant what would you prefer, red meat or white meat?'

Of course, I had no meat preferences. My family was strictly vegetarian and that's how I'd grown up, in blissful ignorance of non-vegetarian culinary delights, except for brief skirmishes with meat in the boy's hostel I went to. Skirmishes, let's just say, that hadn't left me feeling very wholesome about eating it. However, I wasn't going to admit my lack of familiarity with meat to an obvious gourmet.

I shrugged and said, 'Either would do, since I hardly know the difference.' Apparently, it was not the correct response as I noticed his beaming eyes losing their lustre. In an effort to make amends, I said, 'But I am willing to learn.'

The moment I uttered the pacifying promise, I realized that I had made a horrible mistake as I saw his face lighting up. Encouraged, he embarked on taking me, 'a spring chicken', under his non-vegetarian connoisseur wing. He proceeded to explain the difference between red and white, leaving me no choice but to suffer listening to his sermon for the next quarter of an hour, exhibiting the misplaced zeal of a *mullah* (Muslim priest) preaching to a recent convert.

When he finished and went out of my office, I called for my stenographer and asked him how the orderly at the entrance door had permitted someone to barge in unannounced. The stenographer bowed in due deference and said, 'Sir! He is not just "someone". He is the Collector Sahib and everyone knows him to be embarrassingly informal. What do you expect out of an orderly? To stop Alauddin Khilji?'

As I said, from then on almost all Khilji Sahib's interactions with me were directed towards educating me in the subtleties of carnivorous cooking. The lesson during our evening meal at his place was typical of what was to follow. Launching his session, he began,

'Now let me introduce you to red meat, which, I think I forgot to tell you in the morning is not a meeting of communists.' He burst out laughing at his own joke.

When he finished, I replied in the same farcical tone, saying, 'Just as white meat is not a meeting of *firangis* (foreigners). Caucasian ones I mean.' Khilji gave me a quizzical look and in a serious tone said, 'Shekharji, take it from me, Cock-Asian or Amrikan, it is white meat.' Looking suitably contrite, I nodded gravely.

Quite understandably, the segment of his official residence he mostly frequented was the kitchen. Cooking was his pet hobby on weekdays and his occupation on weekends. His office was just a short walking distance from his house and I presume he had a difficult time suppressing his culinary urges to shuffle across from the office to his residence, even as he negotiated the serious business of running a district.

That evening's dinner was mostly mutton (red meat) and I picked at it sketchily enough to give the impression that I was eating it. Even though I praised the dish as delicious, I filled my stomach mostly with the potatoes in the mutton gravy.

On one occasion, after the Chief Minister had presided over a function we had attended at the Birla Institute of Technological Sciences (BITS), Pilani, and had departed for Jaipur, Khilji suggested we travel back together to Jhunjhunu.

As I drove the jeep, he sat next to me holding a loaded 12-bore shotgun vertically reclining on his lap, pointing—mercifully—outwards. The police driver and Khilji's two sidekicks, his personal valet and office clerk, sat at the back and the Collector's vehicle followed behind at a respectful distance.

Though the loaded gun was meant to symbolize Khilji's alertness, in reality, soon after we left Pilani, he had slid into a slouch and dozed off to the soporific drone of the car's engine. Not for long though. At the approach of dusk, his body suddenly shuddered, responding to an in-built alarm, and he sat up with a jerk. His eyes began darting about in an elevated arc, focusing particularly on the branches of trees whizzing past. Then placing a restraining hand on my elbow, he asked me in a hoarse whisper to stop, and even as I treaded softly on the brakes, Khilji aimed and discharged both the barrels on a covey of unsuspecting partridges roosting on a tree. It was not against the law at that time to hunt partridges.

In one blurring swift motion, he put down his gun, snatched an unsheathed knife handed over to him from the back seat and with unbelievable alacrity, climbed down and raced to the spot. His two attachés followed closely behind. Six hapless partridges were laid out within a short distance of each other on the grass. The three of them quicky bundled up the birds and put them in the jeep, their expressions denoting a job well done.

Khilji Sahib, floating on cloud nine, failed to notice my expression of revulsion. He proceeded to educate me, 'This, my friend, is where we will get white meat. And, as you would have noticed, among the six partridges, there is a single black one. A black table-bird is the best variety of white meat.' The sight of him carving them up with his knife had totally put me off and I was in no mood to appreciate his ironical statement of black being the best white. In fact, his action that evening made me take a long sabbatical from non-vegetarianism.

Khilji's day was, however, made. His reputation as an outstanding cook of non-vegetarian cuisine had already spread throughout the state and far outdid his standing as a bureaucrat. Maybe, given the choice, he would have preferred to become the chief chef of a five star hotel rather than the chief administrator of a district.

# 18

# Bonbita

## Prologue

Jalore in 1965 was a sleepy, 'one-horse' town in the south of Rajasthan. It was also a 'one hospital' and 'one doctor' town. She was a gynaecologist who did everything from minor operations to doling out cough syrup and, of course, delivering babies.

Since the last was her primary job, one would have expected her to perform it with ease, but Arjun, our third son, gave her a harrowing time, forcing her to use tougher measures, rather than friendly coaxing, I'm told. When he did finally accept her invitation, he didn't just pop out; halfway, he stopped and looked around curiously at the world as if deciding if it was worth being delivered in. By then, it was too late to contemplate this decision, of course, because the no-nonsense doctor just pulled him out, and not very gently, it's said. He bawled loud and long at the ignominy and was pacified only when he was given to his mother to feed. After finishing his meal and by the time I came into the room, he was gurgling in the most friendly manner,.

These first three things he did on his entry in the world became his signature traits and by the time he became three, he had honed these to near perfection. These traits were: he was curious to the core, friendly to a fault and a gourmand waiting to be feasted.

❧

In 1968, I was posted at Ganganagar, a district well known for its bountiful agricultural land and its violent crime graph, both having a close nexus with each other.

But this story is not about the district; it's about the home of an SP. Among the interesting aspects of being a district SP's family is the presence of a police guard at his residence, complete with a 'sentry box' at the front gate and a 'guard room' at the rear. Mondays and Fridays were prescribed under the rules as 'uniform' days and the guards in full regalia formed up in front of the sentry box to 'present arms' to the SP before he drove to the parade ground.

Twice a week is quite frequent, and constant repetition tends to render even a ceremonial observance into a mechanical routine. Nonetheless, I fondly recall this event for a reason other than the solemn aura of the occasion. This nostalgia is evoked due to my mother's keen participation as an onlooker of the process.

Amma to all, she was an early riser, like all conscientious mothers who are keen to finish their personal chores before the rest of the household wakes up and begins making demands on their time. Never mind the fact that since her daughter-in–law had assumed charge, she had precious little to do but pray for the family and on occasion, lend a hand in the kitchen.

On Mondays and Fridays, Amma would rush through her schedule to the point of even giving short shrift to her deities and risking their wrath. She would settle down on the *muddha* (cane stool) in a lotus pose to ensure that she had a ringside view of the dramatic and colourful ritual of presenting arms by the guard, her eyes agog in anticipation. And I did not let her down. While taking the salute, I could sense her motherly pride egging me on to give a performance to her satisfaction.

Occasionally, Arjun, his eyes still drowsy and blinking, would come and climb onto her lap. Her initial reaction would be to try and unceremoniously shoo him off because he obstructed her vision (she was herself five feet and nothing, in height). Then unable to shake off his stubborn clinging, she would sigh in feigned disgust and make certain adjustments so that both could have a clear view.

Our outdoor instructor at Mount Abu had taken pains to inculcate in us the proper drill for 'saluting' and had emphasized how it was an essential adjunct of a uniformed unit. To describe the salute: It necessitated the triceps of the upper arm were positioned parallel to the ground, maintaining a 45-degree angle between the lower and the upper arm, with the palm turned outwards, straight and flat. No intermediate gaps between the converging fingers and the crook of the thumb are permitted, and the pointing finger lightly rests above the centre of the convex arc protruding from the peak of the police cap.

Unfortunately, there is no dearth of officers who begin to slouch and salute sloppily as their career progresses as if the drill is a frill that can be conveniently dispensed with. It is only internal discipline borne out of love for the uniform that makes some of us persist with doing it right every time.

And, of course, I had the added impetus of Amma's watchful vigil.

Ensconced in the comfort of his grandma's lap, Arjun would find it too difficult to concentrate on the ritual and would inevitably doze off. However, the guard commander's power-packed command, ordering the guard to *Kandhe shastra!* (Shoulder your weapons), would startle Arjun into sitting up wide awake. It was almost as if the burly guard commander was disciplining Arjun too. I could swear there was some connection between them.

Once awake, Arjun and his grandma would stare goggle-eyed as the guard commander continued further with the full-throated command of *Salaami shastra!* (Present arms!) and the entire guard complied in perfect coordination. Then came *Baju shastra!*, signalling the end of the ceremony and time for Amma to go back to the house. I would then mount the jeep and leave for the parade ground. Only Arjun was left to witness the guard commander's final order *Aaraam se*! (At ease). This would also be the cue for Arjun to make the next move.

He would go over to the guards and mingle with them in a friendly way, intrigued by their guns and their shiny boots. Once, I'm told, he went over to the sentry in the box and asked him why he did not join the others during the ceremony. Since the sentry in this particular position was allowed to open his mouth only when called upon to challenge a suspicious-looking stranger with a stern 'Halt! Who goes there? Friend or foe?', and as Arjun was no stranger, the sentry remained silent, staring into vacant space. The guard commander, overhearing the exchange, and by then having dismounted the guard, lifted Arjun on his lap and tried to divert his attention by asking whether the toddler had had his milk yet. He managed to change the topic but not Arjun's habitual curiosity.

Forever thirsting for knowledge, Arjun asked the guard commander what he mixed in his milk, and while the man in uniform struggled to find an appropriate response to the strange query, Arjun volunteered the information that his mother gave him '...Bonbita (Bournvita). You also should have it because she says Bonbita makes a child healthy, wealthy and wise.'

The guard commander's bemused look encouraged Arjun to expand on the topic to include the entire list of food and beverages fed to him all through the day, following which, he asked the guard commander, 'What do you all eat?' The guard commander smiled resignedly and said, 'Bhaiyaji, our meals are sent by the Police Lines. And they are delicious. We have...'

Just then, Arjun's inquisition was cut short by his mother's interruption as she yelled, 'Arjun!' His face grew unhappy at the summons at first, then turned into a smile, when he heard, 'Come and have your milk!'

'Bonbita!' he burst out and ran inside.

His mother and I felt that Arjun, when he turned four, was old enough for some formal schooling and we decided to put him in the same school as his brothers. At first, she was relieved at having some time for herself when Arjun went off to school as his incessant curiosity could be exhausting. But after a while, she began to miss him immensely because he was a challenging sparring partner for her own inquisitive nature.

Her anticipation would begin building up as the time neared for 'the return of the prodigal', an hour ahead of his two brothers. Knowing that he would descend like a starved kitten on the dining table, she timed his arrival to begin laying out piping hot dishes for him.

But to her astonishment, Arjun merely pecked at the food. She was shocked because Arjun had been a healthy eater before he started his school sojourn. When this pattern was repeated for a few days, she got really worried and asked him what the matter was. Arjun said coolly, 'Not hungry.' And that was that.

For him. Not for his parents. When his mother complained for the third time about the drastic drop in his appetite, we decided to consult our general physician. He came over and took Arjun's pulse but when he made a bid to examine the boy with his stethoscope, he more or less failed because Arjun kept giggling and wiggling away from the doctor's prods. Resignedly, the doctor asked him to show his tongue and say 'Aaa', and Arjun responded with a spirited 'Aargh!'

The surprised doctor just about managed to sidestep the spray and did not risk explaining to Arjun the difference between an 'Aaa' and an 'Aargh'. Instead, he put Arjun on the weighing scale. He looked confused and said, 'There seems to be nothing wrong with him. In fact, he has gained weight. Not to worry.'

But worry we did when Arjun continued to peck desultorily at the food day after day. The puzzling thing was the weight gain despite his lunch and dinner going waste. The situation posed a challenge and required a discreet probe. Solving this case became a visceral need because it was eating away at his mother's guts. Our vigil eventually produced results. Our main informer was Man Singh, our family retainer, though it was only when Arjun fell ill that he decided to spill the beans.

These were the facts of the case.

Arjun went to school with his brothers but returned an hour earlier with Man Singh, our faithful retainer, riding pillion on his cycle. Now, as it happened, Arjun's return to our residence coincided with the arrival of the 'meal van' for the guards from the Police Lines. So, while his mother would be busily warming up the food in the kitchen, the guard commander would throw his rank at Man Singh and stealthily scoop up Arjun in his arms, taking him to the guard room, with a weakly protesting Man Singh trailing behind.

Mass-produced police mess food has been the butt of many jokes, the sum and substance of which is that that even a hungry dog would think twice before touching it. The 'butts' are grossly exaggerated. Actually, the food is delicious. However, it's correct that the food is not very conducive to delicate stomachs due to its intense spiciness.

Arjun would partake of the sentrys' meal every day, loving the hot dal (lentils), vegetables coated with gram flour called 'gatte ki sabzi' and other such 'delicacies' of the mess. The guard commander would gently wipe Arjun's nose and eyes as he ate, but these pauses for the wiping process would whet Arjun's appetite, Man Singh told us, and the boy would resume eating with renewed vigour. All the guard members watched the engrossing spectacle in sheer fascination. Paradoxically enough, Arjun's command performance rejuvenated their interest in their own mess food.

Unfortunately, all the spice and chillies in the food finally got to the toddler's formative digestive system. When medicines made no difference to the excruciating stomach ache that the boy had complained of one evening, Man Singh could not bear the sight any longer and decided to reveal all.

The doctor was summoned again and this time, with the boy's symptoms apparent, he felt more confident and on a surer footing. He put the patient through an intensive course of purgatives. Within a few days, Arjun lost weight and his natural verve. He was a pathetic sight to behold and his brothers' faces creased with worry. All the guards came to me with folded hands, standing in a file with bowed heads, looking utterly shattered and apologetic.

I knew that good intentions had gone too far as the guard commander had failed to realize that the mess food was not suitable for children, but in all fairness, he could not have anticipated Arjun's digestive reaction, a reaction that made him go into a deep sleep, perhaps because of the medicines. We all felt helpless, and it was the guard commander who seemed the most distraught. Knowing that he held himself responsible, I tried to put him at ease by asking, 'Do you want see your friend?'

The guard commander nodded eagerly. When he reached Arjun's bed, he bent down and gently touched the sick child's forehead. Then he stood up, ramrod straight. At that point, this mature hunk of a man began howling like a kid. He shed copious tears and began muttering in distress, 'Bhaiyaji, Bhaiyaji.' A pause. 'Bhaiyaji...*aankhe kholo* (open your eyes)'!

And lo and behold, Bhaiyaji complied at once! The guard commander couldn't believe his eyes. 'Sir! Ma'am!' he shouted and beckoned us. Arjun was conscious again! We were all ecstatic at the turn of events. Appropriately, it had been at the beseeching of the guard commander that he had opened his eyes.

Arjun smiled at him, then said 'Bonbita' and pointed at himself.

There was light amidst the gloom in the house. We knew now that Arjun's spell of illness was broken and he was firmly and surely on the way to recovery! His signature traits of friendliness, curiosity and indiscriminate feeding had almost brought him to ruin. But it was also his friend who had brought him back from the brink.

# Acknowledgements

The credit for shaping the text and for making the stories more interesting goes to my son Arjun and I thank him for his valuable contribution. My daughter Shalini added her editorial touch and was an immense support, while my son Bharat deserves thanks for supporting my efforts in dealing with the several versions and generally holding fort at home when I was writing and reviewing the manuscript. Shiela, my muse and wife, helped me recall the details in several of the stories and put up with all the demands I made on her time.

My heartfelt thanks too to Mr K.P.R. Nair for his trust in my ability to curate this collection of cases and for publishing it.

# About the Author

**Rajendra Shekhar** did his schooling at Mayo College, Ajmer and postgraduation in Economics at St Stephen's College, Delhi.

He was selected for the Indian Police Service (IPS), Rajasthan cadre, in 1957. As an IPS officer, he had the rare opportunity to learn and serve in a cadre that was among the most sought-after by IPS probationers.

As the Superintendent of Police (SP) of various districts, he learnt to carry out field work of a high quality and then acquired administrative acumen in various high-profile postings at the police headquarters.

In 1972, he went on deputation to the Central Bureau of Investigation (CBI) and began his assignment in the CBI as SP (Jaipur Branch). In 1975, he was transferred to Delhi on promotion as the

Deputy Inspector General of the CBI. He was in the CBI for about 14 years in different capacities and had the opportunity to supervise many important cases of crime and corruption.

Eventually, he went on to successive postings to head, first, the CBI as the Director and then the Rajasthan state police as the Director General of Police.

He retired from service in October 1992.

He has written four books, three in English and one in Hindi, namely, *Not a Licence to Kill* (Konark Publishers, Delhi), *Defining Moments* (Rupa & Co. Delhi), *Memories are Made of This* (Notion Press, Chennai) and *Pal Ek Pal* (Prabhat Prakashan, Delhi), all of which have drawn good reviews and much appreciation.